VOCABULARY
— FROM —
CLASSICAL
ROOTS

A

Norma Fifer ▾ Nancy Flowers

Educators Publishing Service

Cambridge and Toronto

Acknowledgments

Illustrations in *Vocabulary from Classical Roots—A* have been taken from the following sources:

Catchpenny Prints. 163 Popular Engravings from the Eighteenth Century.
  New York: Dover Publications, Inc., 1970.
1800 Woodcuts by Thomas Bewick and His School. Blanche Cirker, ed.
  New York: Dover Publications, Inc., 1962.
Food and Drink. A Pictorial Archive from Nineteenth-Century Sources.
  Selected by Jim Harter. Third revised edition. New York: Dover
  Publications, Inc., 1983.
Harter's Picture Archive for Collage and Illustration. Jim Harter, ed.
  New York: Dover Publications, Inc., 1978.
Huber, Richard. *Treasury of Fantastic and Mythological Creatures.*
  1,087 Renderings from Historic Sources. New York: Dover
  Publications, Inc., 1981.
The Illustrator's Handbook. Compiled by Harold H. Hart. New York:
  Galahad Books, 1978.
Men. A Pictorial Archive from Nineteenth-Century Sources. Selected
  by Jim Harter. New York: Dover Publications, Inc., 1980.
*More Silhouettes. 868 Copyright-Free Illustrations for Artists and
  Craftsmen.* Carol Belanger Grafton, ed. New York: Dover
  Publications, Inc., 1982.
Rao, Anthony. *The Dinosaur Coloring Book.* New York: Dover
  Publications, Inc., 1982.
Silhouettes. A Pictorial Archive of Varied Illustrations. Carol Belanger
  Grafton, ed. New York: Dover Publications, Inc., 1979.
Tierney, Tom. *Travel and Tourist Illustrations.* New York, Dover
  Publications, Inc., 1987.
2001 Decorative Cuts and Ornaments. Carol Belanger Grafton, ed.
  New York: Dover Publications, Inc., 1988.
*Victorian Spot Illustrations, Alphabets and Ornaments from Porret's Type
  Catalog.* Carol Belanger Grafton, ed. New York: Dover
  Publications, Inc., 1982.

Cover photograph by Katharine Klubock.

Printed in U.S.A.
ISBN 0-8388-2252-5

3 4 5 6 7 VHG 09 08 07 06 05

Contents

Preface

Vocabulary from Classical Roots encourages you to look at words as members of families in the way astronomers see stars as parts of constellations. Here you will become acquainted with constellations of words descended from Greek and Latin, visible in families that cluster around such subjects as the human being, kinds of mental activity, and aspects of daily life.

You will notice that Latin and Greek forms appear as complete words, not as fragments. Some alliances in word families are easily recognizable, but others may seem strange without your seeing the complete sequence of forms. Some Latin words are consistent in their basic forms, like *centum*, "hundred," but others shift in spelling according to the way they are used in Latin sentences: *ars, artis*, "art," and *iter, itineris*, "journey." The principal parts of the verb "to deny" are similar in form: *nego, negare, negavi, nagatum*. But this regularity disappears in the verb "to grow": *cresco, crescere, crevi, cretum*. If you didn't know that these forms belong to one verb, would you believe that the English words *adolescent* and *concrete* belong to the family?

This book can do more than increase your recognition of words; perhaps it will encourage you to study Latin or Greek. More immediately, though, it can remind you that English is a metaphorical language. By returning to the origins of English words you will move closer to knowing how language began: in naming people, things, and concrete actions. So enjoy visualizing the life behind the words you use every day, descendants of Latin and Greek, seeming almost as numerous as stars.

Notes on Using *Vocabulary from Classical Roots*

1. **Latin (L.) and Greek (G.) forms.** Complete sets of these forms help to explain the spelling of their English derivatives. Practice pronouncing these words by following some simple rules.

   To pronounce Latin:
   > Every *a* sounds like *ah*, as in *swan*.
   > The letter *v* is pronounced like *w*.
   > The letter *e* at the end of a word, as in the verb *negare*, should sound like the *e* in *egg*.

   To pronounce Greek:
   > As in Latin, *a* sounds like *ah*.
   > The diphthong *ei* rhymes with *say;* for example, the verb *agein* rhymes with *rain*.
   > *Au*, as in *autos*, sounds like the *ow* in *owl*, and *os* rhymes with *gross*.

2. **Diacritical marks.** Following every defined word in *Vocabulary from Classical Roots* is the guide to pronunciation, as in (dī ə krĭt′ ĭ kəl). The letter that looks like an upside-down *e* (called a *schwa*) is pronounced like the *a* in *about*. You will find a key to the diacritical marks used in this book on the inside front cover.

3. **Derivation.** Information in brackets after the guide to pronunciation for a word gives further information about the source of that word. For example, after **diacritical** (dī ə krĭt′ ĭ kəl), under *dia* <G. "apart," would appear [*krinein* <G. "to separate"]. Thus, the word *diacritical* is made up of two words that come from Greek and means "separating the parts" and, consequently, "distinguishing."

4. **Familiar Words and Challenge Words.** Listed next to groups of defined words may be one or two sets of words belonging to the same family. You probably already know the Familiar Words in the shaded boxes. Try to figure out the meanings of the Challenge Words, and if you are curious, look them up in a dictionary.

5. **Nota Bene.** *Nota bene* means "note well" and is usually abbreviated to *N.B.* In *Vocabulary from Classical Roots,* NOTA BENE calls your attention informally to other words related to the theme of the lesson.

6. **Exercises.** The exercises help you determine how well you have learned the words in each lesson while also serving as practice for examinations such as the SAT: synonyms and antonyms, analogies, and sentence completions. Further exercises illustrate words used in sentences, test recognition of roots, and offer writing practice.

PART ONE

Taking the Measure

Numbers

Directions

1. Determine how the Latin or Greek root is related in meaning and spelling to each defined—KEY—word that follows it.
2. Learn the pronunciation and definition(s) of each KEY word, and notice how the words are used in sentences.
3. Practice using the varied forms of KEY words.
4. Build your knowledge with all the information given: Latin mottoes, Familiar Words, Challenge Words, and Nota Bene references.
5. Complete the exercises.

LESSON 1

E pluribus unum.
One from many.—(Motto of the United States of America)

Key Words		
bilateral	duplicate	monologue
bipartisan	monarch	monopoly
bisect	monogram	unanimous
duplex	monolith	unilateral

MONOS <G. "one"

1. **monologue** (mŏn′ə lôg, mŏn′ə lŏg) [*logos* <G. "word," "speech"] *n.* A long speech made by one performer or by one person in a group.

Because my friend does all the talking, our conversation usually turns into a **monologue**.

2. **monarch**   (mŏn′ərk, mŏn′ärk)   [*arkos* <G. "ruler"]
n. 1. A person who rules a kingdom or empire; a king or queen, emperor or empress.

Queen Victoria was **monarch** of the British Empire at its height.

2. A large black and orange American butterfly.

In early autumn large flocks of **monarchs** migrate from Canada to their winter homes in Mexico.

monarchial, *adj.*; **monarchic**, *adj.*; **monarchical**, *adj.*; **monarchy**, *n.*

3. **monogram**   (mŏn′ə grăm)   [*gramma* <G. "letter"]
n. A design composed of letters, usually the first letter of a name.

The personal dishes and silverware of French monarch Napoleon Bonaparte bore the **monogram** N.

monogram, *v.*

4. **monopoly**   (mə nŏp′ə lē)   [*polein* <G. "to sell"]
n. 1. Exclusive control of the trade in some item or service.

One publisher holds a **monopoly** on printing all of our school publications.

2. Sole ownership or control of anything.

During the winter the basketball team has a **monopoly** on the gym after school.

monopolize, *v.*

5. **monolith**   (mŏn′ə lĭth)   [*lithos* <G. "stone"]
n. 1. A large block of stone.

A massive **monolith** formed the roof of the tomb.

2. A large organization that acts as a single unit.

Local restaurants cannot compete with a **monolith** like a national fast-food chain.

monolithic, *adj.*

Familiar Words
inch
onion
ounce
unicorn
unicycle
uniform
unify
unique
unit
universal
union
unite
universe
university

Challenge Words
unicameral
unicellular
unisex
unison
Unitarian
unitary
univalent

UNUS < L. "one"

6. **unanimous** (yōō năn′ə məs) [*animus* <L. "mind," "spirit"]
adj. Being in complete agreement.

To reach a verdict, a jury must achieve a **unanimous** decision.

unanimity, *n.*; **unanimously**, *adv.*

7. **unilateral** (yōō′nə lăt′ər əl) [*latus* <L. "side"]
adj. One-sided; done by or affecting one person, group, or country, etc., and not another.

Since the rest of my family was away when the house burned, I had to make **unilateral** decisions about repairs.

unilaterally, *adv.*

NOTA BENE: It is easy to see how some words are derived from *unus*; for example; a unicorn ("one" plus *cornu*, "horn") is a mythical beast with only one horn. But how is *onion* related to *unus*? Slice an onion crosswise and see the answer. Concentric circles, one inside the other, account for the word's derivation from *unus*. Words like *inch* and *ounce* have undergone several changes in form since ancient Roman times; earlier versions of these words were more similar to *unus* than our modern words.

Familiar Word
double

Challenge Words
doublet
doubloon
duplicity
duple

DUO <L. "two"
DUPLEX <L. "twofold"

8. **duplex** (dōō′plĕks, dyōō′plĕks) [*duplex* <L. "twofold"]
n. A dwelling with two living units.

The two families living in the **duplex** shared the same front porch and back yard.

9. **duplicate** (dōō′plĭ kāt, dyōō′plĭ kāt) [*plicare* <L. "to fold"]
tr. v. To make an identical copy or double of something; to repeat.

Forgers try to **duplicate** precisely the paper, design, and engraving techniques of genuine currency.

duplicate, *adj.*; **duplicate**, *n.*; **duplicating**, *adj.*

<table>
<tr><td>

Familiar Words
biceps
bicultural
bicycle
bifocals
bilingual
billion
bimonthly
binoculars
biracial
biweekly

</td></tr>
</table>

<table>
<tr><td>

Challenge Words
biannual
bicameral
bicarbonate
bicentennial
bicuspid
biennial
bifurcate
binomial
biped
biplane
bipolar
bivalve

</td></tr>
</table>

BI <L. "two"

10. bilateral (bī lăt′ər əl) [*latus* <L. "side"]
adj. 1. Having two sides.

Our school has a **bilateral** athletic program that includes both in-school and after-school sports.

2. Made between two persons or groups.

Canada and the United States have a **bilateral** trade agreement.

bilaterally, *adv.*

11. bipartisan (bī pär′tĭ zən) [*pars, partis* <L. "part"]
adj. Involving two political parties.

The hearings, conducted by both Republicans and Democrats, reflected the **bipartisan** approach.

12. bisect (bī′sĕkt′, bī′sĕkt′) [*secare* <L. "to cut"]
tr. v. To divide into two equal parts.

When you **bisect** a square, you end up with two rectangles.

bisection, *n.*

EXERCISE 1A   Circle the letter of the best SYNONYM (the word or phrase most nearly the same as the word(s) in bold-faced type).

1. submit applications in **duplicate**   a. twice   (b.) in two identical copies   c. on time   d. several times   e. bilaterally

2. a(n) **unilateral** offer   a. sideways   b. unfair   c. agreed upon   d. awkward   (e.) one-sided

3. to **bisect** a field   a. plow   (b.) halve   c. dig into   d. cross   e. duplicate

4. a **bipartisan** effort   a. Republican   b. two-sided   c. halfhearted   (d.) two-party   e. divided

5. a pink **duplex**   a. design of two letters   b. single-family house   c. apartment building   d. sheet of plastic   (e.) two-family house

6. an elaborate **monogram**   a. large stone   (b.) design of letters   c. long speech   d. throne   e. skit

Circle the letter of the best ANTONYM (the word or phrase most nearly opposite the word in bold-faced type).

7. our **unanimous** opinion   (a.) divided   b. anonymous   c. united
   d. secret   e. honest

8. a **monolithic** institution   a. Stone Age   (b.) fragmented   c. concrete
   d. unified   e. solid

9. **monopolize** the resources   a. save   b. waste   (c.) equally share
   d. increase   e. develop

EXERCISE 1B   Circle the letter of the sentence in which the word in bold-faced type is used incorrectly.

1. a. After World War I Germany was no longer ruled by its **monarch**, Kaiser Wilhelm, but by an elected assembly.
   b. **Monarchs** feed on milkweed plants.
   c. On the door of the limousine was the royal crest and *ERII*, the **monarch** of Queen Elizabeth II of England.
   (d.) When the American colonies won independence from England, some people wanted to establish a **monarchy** with George Washington as king.

2. a. In *The Belle of Amherst* an actress delivers a **monologue** as Emily Dickinson.
   b. Don't ask how she's been, or we'll get a twenty-minute **monologue** on her trip to China.
   c. The comedian's hilarious **monologue** was about life in a small town.
   (d.) Romeo and Juliet pledge their love in a romantic **monologue** during the balcony scene.

3. a. The novel *1984* describes a dreary world in which a **monolithic** government represses all individual rights.
   b. Stonehenge, a circle of standing **monoliths**, may have been used as a kind of solar observatory.
   (c.) Human beings in the **monolithic** period had not yet discovered the uses of fire.
   d. In an attempt to personalize the **monolithic** corporation, the new president regularly visited workers and invited their suggestions.

4. (a.) In a **monopoly**, power is held on the basis of majority rule.
   b. One student seems to **monopolize** every class discussion.
   c. During the eighteenth century the British held an absolute **monopoly** on trade with the American colonies.
   d. By gaining a **monopoly** in the steel industry, a few financiers virtually controlled the nation's economy.

5. ⓐ Five rivers **bisect** the plains.
   b. The estate is **bisected** by an irrigation canal.
   c. When you **bisect** an angle of 90°, two 45° angles are produced.
   d. **Bisecting** an irregular area precisely is difficult.
6. ⓐ Our school has a **bilateral** antismoking campaign that encourages smokers to quit and warns nonsmokers never to start.
   b. Poland, Latvia, and Estonia entered into a **bilateral** alliance.
   c. In **bilateral** discussions, both union and management agreed to compromise their demands.
   d. The two cousins worked out a **bilateral** arrangement to share the family sailboat on alternate weekends.

EXERCISE 1C   Fill in each blank with the most appropriate word from Lesson 1. Use a word or any of its forms only once.

1. Queen Liliuokalani, the nineteenth-century ___monarch___ of the Hawaiian Islands, wrote the famous song "Aloha Oe."

2. In *The Odyssey*, banquet guests listen in silent fascination to the hero Odysseus's ___monologue___ about his adventurous return from the Trojan War.

3. A handkerchief with the ___monogram___ M.M. was found at the scene of the crime.

4. Since everyone loves to skate, the vote to hold our class party at the rink was ___unanimous___.

5. The committee said that it wanted to refrain from ___unilateral___ action and therefore hoped the disputing parties could resolve the conflict among themselves.

6. The neighbors made a ___bipartisan___ agreement to pay equally to build a fence between their two houses.

7. The Republican senators' willingness to work with the Democrats indicates their ___bilateral___ approach to solving problems.

8. Although it contains two separate apartments, the building did not appear on the outside to be a ___duplex___.

LESSON 2

Gallia est omnis divisa in partes tres.
All Gaul is divided into three parts.—JULIUS CAESAR

Key Words

bicentennial	decimate	quatrain
centenary	quadrant	trilogy
centigrade	quartet	trisect
decathlon		triumvirate

Familiar Words
tricycle
trillion
trimester
trio
triple
triplet
triplicate

Challenge Words
tricentennial
trident
triennial
trinity
tripartite
triplex
triptych

TRI <G. "three"
TRES <L. "three"

1. **trilogy**   (trĭl'ə jē)   [*logos* <G. "word," "speech"]
   n. A group of three literary or musical works that have a related theme.

   The *Lord of the Rings*, Tolkien's popular **trilogy**, contains these novels: *The Fellowship of the Ring*, *The Two Towers*, and *The Return of the King*.

2. **trisect**   (trī'sĕkt, trī sĕkt')   [*secare* <L. "to cut"]
   tr. v. To divide into three parts.

   The two freeways **trisected** the once-united community into three separate neighborhoods.

   trisection, *n.*; **trisector**, *n.*

3. **triumvirate**   (trī ŭm'vər ĭt)   [*triumviri* <L. "board of three" <L. *vir*, "man"]
   n. A group of three, especially in authority.

   In ancient Rome the Second **Triumvirate** was composed of Mark Anthony, Augustus Caesar, and Lepidus.

QUARTUS <L. "fourth"
QUATUOR <L. "four"

4. **quadrant**   (kwŏd'rənt)
   n. 1. (mathematics) A quarter of a circle or of its circumference.

   A **quadrant** contains 90 degrees of the 360 degrees of a circle.

Familiar Words
quadrangle
quadruple
quadruplet
quart
quarter
squad
square

Challenge Words
quadraphonic
quadrennial
quadrille
quadripartite
quarry
quarto
quatrefoil

2. An early machine for measuring altitudes.

Although primitive, the **quadrant** enabled explorers to take accurate measurements.

3. Any of the four parts of an area divided by perpendicular lines.

Rescuers divided the forest into **quadrants** and searched each thoroughly for survivors.

5. **quartet** (kwôr tět′)
n. 1. A musical composition for four voices or instruments.

Most operas contain a **quartet** for two women (a soprano and an alto) and two men (a tenor and a bass).

2. A set of four, especially of four musicians.

During the complicated heart operation, a **quartet** of surgeons worked for ten hours.

6. **quatrain** (kwŏt′rān′, kwŏ′trān′)
n. A stanza or group of four lines of poetry.

Most nursery rhymes, like "Little Bo Peep Has Lost Her Sheep," are written in **quatrains**.

NOTA BENE: *Pente* and *quinque* are both roots that mean "five." They appear in many words. *Pente*, for example, is the root in *pentagon*, "a five-sided figure," and *pentathlon*, "an Olympic event testing five different skills." *Quinque* is the root for words like *quintet*, "a group of five," and *quintuplets*, "five babies born to one mother at the same time."

You will recognize the roots *sex, septem, octo,* and *novem,* which mean "six," "seven," "eight," and "nine" respectively, in many familiar words. For example, *September, October,* and *November* were the seventh, eighth, and ninth months of the Roman calendar.

Combined with the root *-ginta,* which means "ten times," they form the words to indicate a person whose age is between 60 and 70, a *sexagenarian;* between 70 and 80, a *septuagenarian;* between 80 and 90, an *octogenarian;* and between 90 and 100, a *nonagenarian.*

Combined with the root *plus,* which means "fold," these roots make *sextuple, septuple, octuple,* and *nonuple,* indicating six, seven, eight, or nine times.

Familiar Words
decade
December
decimal

Challenge Words
decagram
Decalogue
deciliter
decimeter
duodecimal

DECEM <L. "ten"

7. decimate   (dĕs'ə māt)
tr. v. 1. To destroy a large part of.

European diseases like measles **decimated** Native American populations because they had no immunity.

2. To kill one in every ten.

To punish a legion that had shown cowardice, the Roman army sometimes **decimated** soldiers of all ranks on the basis of a lottery.

decimation, *n.*

8. decathlon   (dĭ kăth'lən, dĭ kăth'lŏn)   [*athlon* <G. "contest"]
n. An athletic contest in which each contestant takes part in ten events.

The winner of the Olympic **decathlon** can be considered an all-around athlete.

NOTA BENE: Several Olympic competitions combine several sports. In the *biathlon* athletes compete in two sports: cross-country skiing and rifle shooting. The five sports of the *pentathlon* are usually running, fencing, swimming, horseback riding, and pistol shooting. The *decathlon* includes ten track and field events.

Familiar Words
cent
centennial
centimeter
centipede
century
percent

Challenge Words
centavo
centenarian
centiliter
centime

CENTUM <L. "hundred"

9. bicentennial   (bī'sĕn tĕn'ē əl)   [*bi* <L. "two"; *annus* <L. "year"]
n. A two-hundredth anniversary.

In 1989 the **bicentennial** of the first ten amendments to the U.S. Constitution, the Bill of Rights, was celebrated.

adj. Happening every 200 years.

As part of **bicentennial** events honoring the French Revolution, the Louvre, the great Parisian museum, was enlarged in 1988.

bicentennially, *adv.*

10. centenary   (sĕn tĕn'ə rē, sĕn'tə nĕr´ ē)
adj. Pertaining to a 100-year period.

Our town is preparing a time capsule of contemporary articles to be opened at its next **centenary** celebration.

n. A centennial.

By its first **centenary** Boston's population had tripled.

11. **centigrade** (sĕn´tĭ grād´) [*gradus* <L. "step"] *adj.* Referring to a thermometer scale of 100 degrees where water freezes at 0° and boils at 100°.

Although most Americans continue to use the Fahrenheit scale where water freezes at 32° and boils at 212°, scientists use the **centigrade** scale because it makes calculations easier.

EXERCISE 2A

Circle the letter of the best SYNONYM (the word or phrase most nearly the same as the word in bold-faced type).

1. reached **0° centigrade**   a. freezing   b. boiling   c. 100° Fahrenheit   d. 212° Fahrenheit   e. the melting point
2. to **decimate** the population   a. slaughter   b. increase   c. infect   d. educate   e. unite
3. a lyric **quatrain**   a. courtyard   b. party of four   c. dance for four   d. four-line verse   e. four-week period
4. occur **bicentennially**   a. every two years   b. every 200 years   c. twice in 100 years   d. twice in 200 years   e. every 2000 years
5. a(n) **centenary** celebration   a. surprise   b. annual   c. bicentennial   d. one-sided   e. hundredth anniversary
6. controlled by a **triumvirate**   a. noble person   b. triplet   c. dictator   d. group of three people   e. trilogy
7. applaud the **quartet**   a. dancers   b. orchestra   c. pair of cellists   d. chorus   e. four performers

EXERCISE 2B

Fill in each blank with a word from Lesson 2. Use a word only once.

1. 3 closely related musical works = _____
2. 3 political leaders = _____
3. 4 people playing musical instruments = _____
4. 4 lines of poetry = _____
5. 10 track and field events = _____
6. scale of 100 degrees = _____
7. 200 years = _____

EXERCISE 2C   Fill in each blank with the most appropriate word from Lesson 2. Use a word or any of its forms only once.

1. Ursula LeGuin's *The Earthsea* _____ contains three separate novels involving the same characters in different stages of their lives.

2. One of the most grueling events of the Olympics, the _____ requires skill in ten different sports.

3.   "I never saw a purple cow,
          I never hope to see one.
          But I can tell you, anyhow,
          I'd rather see than be one."—Gelett Burgess

   This nonsense verse is an example of a _____.

4. The monarch's three children _____ed the realm among themselves.

5. Antarctic explorers carried a _____ in order to determine the altitude of newly discovered peaks.

6. Decisions at our school are generally made by the _____ of principal, vice-principal, and dean of students.

7. I wonder how the first moon landing will be regarded at its

   _____ in 2169.

8. A barbershop _____ usually sings popular songs in harmony for four voices.

9. Until whales were protected by international treaties, excessive

   hunting nearly _____d them.

REVIEW EXERCISES FOR LESSONS 1 AND 2

1 Fill in the blank or circle the letter of the best answer.

1. Both the Greek root _____ and the Latin root

_____ mean "one."

NOTA BENE: The following exercise is an *analogy*, a statement of relationship between two elements. In this kind of exercise one pair is compared to another, as in a mathematical ratio:
  2 : 4 :: 5 : 10 (which should be read "2 is to 4 as 5 is to 10").
  Some analogies combine words and numbers:
    penny : dime :: 1 : 10
    2 : bisect :: 3 : trisect
Most of the analogies in this book compare words only and ask you to find a pair among five choices that best matches the first pair, for example,
    monarch : Queen Elizabeth II ::
    a. Napoleon : emperor
    b. captain : team
    c. director : play
    d. congressperson : senator
    e. president : Franklin D. Roosevelt
(The answer is *e*.)

2. duplex : two ::
  a. one : monopoly
  b. decimate : hundred
  c. triumvirate : three
  d. unilateral : bilateral
  e. three : trilogy
3. *monos* : one ::
  a. *tri* : *bi*
  b. *unus* : one
  c. *quartus* : fifth
  d. ten : *decem*
  e. *unus* : *monos*
4. trisect : bisect ::
  a. unity : unanimity
  b. 2 : 3
  c. 3 : 2
  d. monogram : trilogy
  e. multiply : divide

5. The Latin roots _____ and_____ both mean "two."

6. Using your knowledge of words and roots in Lessons 1 and 2, explain what you think these words mean (the words marked with * are not in most dictionaries).

    a. trilateral _____

    b. quadrasect* _____

    c. decacentennial*_____

    d. centuplicate* _____

    e. triplex _____

2 Writing or Discussion Activities

1. Use each pair of words in a sentence.
    a. monopolize—monologue
    b. unanimous—triumvirate

2. Imagine that a committee in your school, described by the school paper as bipartisan, meets to discuss some local problem. What might be the problem and what groups might make up the two "parties" on this bipartisan committee? Use *bipartisan* in your response.

3. Describe in a few sentences a situation that can be described as either *unilateral* or *bilateral*. Let your description make clear why the word is appropriate to that situation. Use one of those words in your description.

4. Write a monologue in which one of these speakers describes a relationship.
    a. the ruler of a monolithic monarchy who is lonesome for a friend
    b. the owner of one side of a duplex shared with very noisy neighbors
    c. a member of a triumvirate plotting to get rid of the other two
    d. a member of a quartet who feels superior to the other three

All or Nothing

LESSON 3

Omne corpus mutabile est.
Every object is subject to change.—CICERO

Key Words

catholic	omnipresent	pandemonium
cloister	omnivorous	preclude
holocaust	panacea	recluse
omnipotent		totalitarian

Familiar Words
Pan-American
pancreas
panorama

PAN <G. "all"

1. **pandemonium**   (păn´ də mō´nē əm)
   [*daimon* <G. "divine power"]
   n. Uproar.

   Pandemonium threatens to break out after Julius Caesar is assassinated on the ides of March, but in Shakespeare's play Brutus calms the murderous senators.

2. **panacea** (păn´ə sē´ə)   [*akos* <G. "cure"]
n. A cure-all for diseases or troubles.

Some politicians seem to regard tax cuts as a **panacea** for economic problems.

OMNIS <L. "all"

3. **omnipotent** (ŏm nĭp´ə tənt)
[*potens* <L. *posse*, "to be able"]
adj. Having unlimited power; all-powerful.

To the ancient British tribes the invading Roman army seemed **omnipotent**.

omnipotence, *n.*; **the Omnipotent**, *n.*; **omnipotently**, *adv.*

4. **omnipresent** (ŏm´nĭ prĕz´ənt)
adj. Present everywhere.

At harvest time the smell of garlic is **omnipresent** in Gilroy, California, "the garlic capital of America."

5. **omnivorous** (ŏm nĭv´ər əs)   [*vorare* <L. "to devour"]
adj. 1. Feeding on both plants and meat.

Human beings are **omnivorous**, though many choose to be vegetarians.

2. Devouring everything, especially intellectually.

She is such an **omnivorous** reader she has already read all of the library's biographies, science fiction, and sports magazines.

omnivore, *n.*; **omnivorously**, *adv.*; **omnivorousness**, *n.*

HOLOS <G. "whole"

6. **catholic** (kăth´ə lĭk, kăth´lĭk)   [*kata-* <G. "according to"]
adj. 1. Universal; including most things.

Her wide travels reflect her **catholic** tastes.

2. (capitalized) Referring to the Roman Catholic church.

Spain is a predominantly **Catholic** country.

catholic, *n.*; **catholically**, *adv.*

7. **holocaust**   (hō′lə kôst, hŏl′ə kôst)
   [*kaustos* <G. "burned"]
   n. 1. A great destruction, especially by fire.

   After the great 1906 earthquake, a **holocaust** swept through San Francisco.

   2. (capitalized) Murder by the Nazis of over six million Jews and millions of other people in World War II.

   Most Americans first learned of the extent of the **Holocaust** when the Nazi concentration camps were liberated at the end of World War II.

   holocaustal, *adj.*; **holocaustic**, *adj.*

TOTUS <L. "whole"

8. **totalitarian**   (tō tăl′ ĭ târ′ē ən)   [*total* + (author) *itarian*]
   adj. Referring to a form of government in which one person or party holds absolute control.

   Under Joseph Stalin the Soviet Union became a **totalitarian** state.

   totalitarianism, *n.*

CLAUDO, CLAUDERE, CLAUSI, CLAUSUM <L. "to close"

9. **cloister**   (kloi′stər)
   n. 1. A covered walk along the inside walls of a building, usually looking out on a courtyard.

   The **cloister** of the country house provided a welcome protection from the tropical sun.

   2. A monastery or similar place of religious seclusion.

   During the Reformation many **cloisters** were closed and their monks or nuns dispersed.

   tr. v. To seclude as in a monastery.

   To protect their children from the Black Plague, the parents **cloistered** them in an isolated village.

   cloistered, *adj.*

10. **preclude** (prĭ klo͞od′) [*pre* <L. "before"]
    tr. v. To prevent; to make impossible.

    Rain **precluded** our taking a walk.

    preclusion, *n.*; **preclusive**, *adj.*

11. **recluse** (rĕk′lo͞os, rĕ klo͞os′) [*re* <L. intensifier]
    n. A person who avoids mixing with people.

    The **recluse** preferred the company of a dog and the library to that of people.

    reclusion, *n.*; **reclusive**, *adj.*

EXERCISE 3A   Circle the letter of the best SYNONYM (the word or phrase most nearly the same as the word in bold-faced type).

1. a(n) **omnipresent** fear   a. ever-present   b. paralyzing
   c. unilateral   d. decimating   e. foolish
2. to oppose **totalitarianism**   a. complete control by one person
   b. unity   c. common goals   d. peace   e. unanimity
3. seeking a **panacea** a. snack   b. cure-all   c. small cooking utensil
   d. place of protection   e. general opinion
4. a(n) **omnivorous** beast   a. meat-eating   b. grass-eating   c. shy
   d. starving   e. plant- and meat-eating

Circle the letter of the best ANTONYM (the word or phrase most nearly opposite the word in bold-faced type).

5. circumstances **preclude** the launch   a. make possible   b. keep secret
   c. postpone   d. make public   e. prevent
6. having **catholic** interests   a. Protestant   b. vague   c. unilateral
   d. religious   e. democratic
7. a(n) **reclusive** disposition   a. daring   b. demanding   c. outgoing
   d. thrifty   e. exclusive
8. a(n) **omnipotent** army   a. undetermined   b. forceful
   c. well-trained   d. ignorant   e. defenseless
9. **pandemonium** in the class   a. hostility   b. quiet   c. disobedience
   d. holocaust   e. excitement

EXERCISE 3B   Circle the letter of the sentence in which the word in bold-faced type is used incorrectly.

1. a. Apes are **omnivorous**, eating fruit, roots, leaves, insects, and occasionally the flesh of other animals.
    b. A true **omnivore** excels at both sports and academics.
    c. **Omnivores** have both sharp teeth for tearing flesh and flat teeth for grinding grains.
    d. She is an **omnivorous** collector of baseball cards; she spends all of her allowance on her collection and then begs her parents for more money.

2. a. Don't **cloister** your emotions: express what you feel.
    b. **Cloistered** in an over-protective family, he grew up unaware of social problems.
    c. The **cloister** protects monks from bad weather as they pass from their dormitory to the chapel for midnight services.
    d. In the Middle Ages unmarried females were sometimes **cloistered** for life by their families.

3. a. Lightning set off a **holocaust** that destroyed the whole village.
    b. The concentration camp at Dachau has been converted to a memorial to the victims of the **Holocaust**.
    c. An old-fashioned barbecue requires **holocausting** an entire cow overnight.
    d. Popular legend blames the nineteenth-century **holocaust** that destroyed Chicago on Mrs. O'Leary's cow, which kicked over a lantern in the barn.

4. a. **Catholics** recognize the Pope as the head of their church.
    b. Beatrix Potter's stories like "Peter Rabbit," which has been translated into many languages, have **catholic** appeal to small children.
    c. Despite their **Catholic** upbringing, they had very narrow interests and opinions.
    d. Because he is so **catholic** in his interests, he had difficulty choosing a subject to major in at college.

EXERCISE 3C   Fill in each blank with the most appropriate word from Lesson 3. Use a word or any of its forms only once.

1. When penicillin was first developed in the 1940s, many doctors

   regarded it as a _____ that would end all infectious diseases.

2. Although Elizabeth Barrett's family regarded her as a _____ too fragile to tolerate company, she eloped with fellow poet Robert Browning and led a vigorous family life.

3. In *Night* Elie Wiesel records how he survived the _____ as a twelve-year-old Jewish boy in a Nazi concentration camp.

4. Originally regarded as a god with absolute authority over the Aztecs,

   Montezuma's reputation for _____ was destroyed by the Spanish invasion.

5. Because we had held so many drills, there was no _____ when a real fire broke out, and everyone left the building calmly.

6. Although Rapunzel was _____ed in a high tower to hide her beauty, her long hair served as a ladder for her rescuer.

7. As the team dressed before the track meet, tension was

   _____ in the locker room.

LESSON 4

Humani nihil a me alienum puto.
I think nothing human is alien to me.—TERENCE.

Key Words		
annihilate	negate	renegade
aperture	nihilism	vacuous
inception	overt	vanity
incipient		vaunt

Challenge Word
incipit

INCIPIO, INCIPERE, INCEPI, INCEPTUM <L. "to begin"

1. **inception**   (ĭn sĕp′shən)
   n. The beginning of something.

   Since the **inception** of a vaccine for polio, that disease has almost disappeared from the earth.

2. **incipient**   (ĭn sĭp′ē ənt)
   adj. In its early stages; beginning.

   A sore throat and runny nose are the symptoms of an **incipient** cold.

   incipiently, *adv.*

NIHIL <L. "nothing"

3. **annihilate**   (ə nī′ə lāt′)   [*an* = *ad* <L. "to"]
   tr. v. To destroy completely.

   During the radio broadcast of *The War of the Worlds*, thousands of listeners thought Martians were about to **annihilate** New Jersey.

   annihilable, *adj.*; **annihilation**, *n.*; **annihilator**, *n.*
   Synonym: **decimate**

4. **nihilism**   (nī′ə lĭz′əm, nī′hə lĭz′əm, nē′ə lĭz əm)
   n. The total rejection of religious or moral beliefs.

   From the point of view of **nihilism**, any behavior is acceptable since no rules of ethics exist.

   nihilist, *n.*; **nihilistic**, *adj.*; **nihility**, *n.*

NEGO, NEGARE, NEGAVI, NEGATUM <L. "to deny"

5. **negate**   (nĭ gāt′)
   tr. v. 1. To disprove; to nullify.

   Columbus's voyage to the New World **negated** the theory that the earth was flat.

   2. To rule out; to cancel; to repeal.

   The legislation allowing eighteen year olds to vote **negated** previous laws that had set the voting age at twenty-one or older.

   negation, *n.*

6. **renegade**   (rĕn′ ĭ gād)   [*re* <L. intensifier]
   n. One who deserts a group, cause, faith, etc.; an outlaw.

   When Democrats lost the election, many former supporters turned **renegade** and joined the Republicans.

   adj. Like a renegade; traitorous.

   Loyal troops crushed the revolt and imprisoned **renegade** officers.

VANUS <L. "empty"
VACUUS <L. "empty"

7. **vacuous**   (văk′yo͞o əs)
   adj. Empty, especially of meaning or purpose.

Familiar Words
avoid
evacuate
vain
vacation
vacuum
void

Challenge Words
devoid
vacate

Educators often criticize television cartoons for kids as **vacuous** entertainment.

vacuity, *n.*

8. **vanity** (văn′ ĭ tē)
n. 1. Conceit, especially about one's appearance.

Despite the **vanity** of the Spanish royal family, Francisco Goya painted their portraits showing all their physical and moral shortcomings.

2. Something worthless or useless.

Buddhism teaches that human ambitions are **vanity**.

3. A dressing table.

A **vanity** usually has an attached mirror and many drawers.

9. **vaunt** (vônt, vŏnt)
tr. v. To boast; to brag about.

Gracious winners do not **vaunt** their victories.

n. A boast.

Parents′ **vaunts** about their possessions often embarrass their children.

vaunted, *adj.*

Familiar Word
overture

Challenge Word
apéritif

APERIO, APERIRE, APERUI, APERTUM <L. "to open"

10. **aperture** (ăp′ər chər)
n. An opening, especially one that admits light.

The photographer adjusted the **aperture** of the lens to let in more light.

11. **overt** (ō vûrt′, ō′vûrt′)
adj. Done or shown openly.

Their **overt** hostility gave us little hope for a reconciliation.

overtly, *adv.*

EXERCISE 4A   Circle the letter of the best SYNONYM (the word or phrase most nearly
the same as the word in bold-faced type).

1. **overt** aggressions   a. preclusive   b. fierce   c. obvious
   d. bipartisan   e. conscious
2. find no **aperture**   a. opportunity   b. clue   c. excuse   d. cloister
   e. opening
3. a(n) **vacuous** conversation   a. boring   b. innocent   c. overt
   d. meaningful   e. pointless

Circle the letter of the best ANTONYM (the word or phrase most nearly
opposite the word in bold-faced type).

4. the **incipient** storm   a. dramatic   b. anticipated   c. annihilating
   d. concluding   e. rain
5. a **renegade** soldier   a. valiant   b. boastful   c. faithful   d. veteran
   e. wounded
6. the **inception** of their romance   a. conception   b. purpose
   c. break-up   d. rumor   e. mistake

EXERCISE 4B   Circle the letter of the sentence in which the word in bold-faced type is
used incorrectly.

1. a. Disillusioned with the **vacuous** vanities of court life, John Donne
      became a priest.
   b. I prefer a book to the **vacuous** conversation at most parties.
   c. In many works of science fiction a human being becomes lost in
      the immense **vacuity** of outer space.
   d. The **vacuity** created by hundreds of suction cups on an octopus's
      tentacles enables it to hold fast to rocks.
2. a. **Vanity** made Queen Elizabeth I prey to flatterers.
   b. In *Pilgrim's Progress* the hero is tempted to linger on his journey
      at Vanity Fair, where all the **vanities** of the world can be
      purchased.
   c. It is **vanity** to think you can change human nature.
   d. Reluctant to **vanity** her fame, she travels modestly under an
      assumed name.
3. a. To a **nihilist**, patriotism makes no sense.
   b. The Russian Czar regarded **nihilistic** ideas as a threat to the
      monarchy.
   c. **Nihilism** rejects education on the grounds that we can never
      learn anything anyway.
   d. After years of extravagant living beyond their budget, they faced
      nihilism.

4. a. The research of Polish astronomer Copernicus **negated** the long-held theory that the sun moved around the earth.
   b. A **negate** like her criticizes everything and approves nothing.
   c. An atheist **negates** the existence of God; an agnostic remains uncertain.
   d. This treaty **negates** all previous alliances the nations had made.

EXERCISE 4C   Fill in each blank with the most appropriate word from Lesson 4. Use a word or any of its forms only once.

1. All wildlife was _____d by the forest fire.

2. We grew weary of hearing her _____ her athletic achievements.

3. Since its _____ in 1945, the United Nations has been the subject of controversy.

4. The new students were easily identifiable by their _____ self-consciousness on the first day of school.

5. Smoke from the cooking fire escaped through an _____ at the top of the tepee.

6. A _____ believes that neither ethical nor religious rules can govern human behavior.

7. Education reformer Maria Montessori encouraged kindergarteners'

   _____ interest in arithmetic by providing games for weighing and measuring.

8. Following the American Civil War, Southern farmers were often

   threatened by "bushwhackers," _____ soldiers who had deserted the army to becoming roving bandits.

REVIEW EXERCISES FOR LESSONS 3 AND 4

1 Fill in the blank or circle the letter of the best answer.

1. Both the Greek root _____ and the Latin root _____ mean "all."
2. pandemonium : uproar ::
   a. cloister : catholic
   b. omnivorous : meat-eating
   c. Catholic : Holocaust
   d. preclude : prevent
   e. vacuous : omnipresent
3. *claudere* : *aperire* ::
   a. *omnis* : *totus*
   b. *vanus* : *vacuus*
   c. to close : to open
   d. *incipere* : begin
   e. door : aperture
4. *nihil* : *omnis*
   a. *pan* : *holos*
   b. all : nothing
   c. nothing : all
   d. *totus* : *omnis*
   e. never : always

5. Both the root _____ and the root _____ mean "empty."

6. *Negare* means _____ .

2 Writing or Discussion Activities

1. Write two sentences showing the different meanings of *catholic*.
2. Write sentences in which you use any two words from each group:
   a. omnipotence, vaunt, overt
   b. vanity, preclude, incipient
3. Write a sentence or two in which you describe someone's vacuous behavior. Use *vacuous* or *vacuity* in your sentence.
4. Write a sentence or two in which you try to explain why someone might become a recluse. Use *recluse* in your sentence.

LESSONS 5 AND 6

More or Less

LESSON 5

Satis eloquentiae, sapientiae parum.
Enough eloquence, too little wisdom.

Key Words

attenuate	microbe	minutia
comply	microcosm	replete
expletive	minuscule	satiate
implement		tenuous

MIKROS <G. "small"

1. **microbe** (mī′krōb) [*bios* <G. "life"]
   n. An organism invisible to the naked
   eye, especially one that causes disease.

   Malaria is caused by a **microbe** that can be
   transmitted by the bite of certain mosquitoes.

2. **microcosm**   (mī′krə kŏz′əm)   [*kosmos* <G. "universe"]
n. A miniature world; something that resembles something else on a very small scale.

A school community is a **microcosm** of the whole society in which it exists.

microcosmic, *adj.*

MINUO, MINUERE, MINUI, MINUTUM <L. "to lessen"
MINUS <L. "less"

3. **miniscule**   (mĭn′ə skyōōl′)
adj. Extremely small.

The dollhouse was furnished in every detail, including **miniscule** silverware and napkin rings.

4. **minutia**   (mĭ nōō′shē ə, mĭ nōō′shə, mĭ nyōō′shə;
plural **minutiae:** mĭ nōō′shē ē′)
n. A small or trivial detail.

A seemingly insignificant **minutia**—like a fragment of bone or a pottery chip—can yield important information at an archeological site.

TENUO, TENUARE, TENUAVI,
TENUATUM <L. "to make thin"
TENUIS <L. "thin"

5. **attentuate**   (ə ten′yōō āt)   [*at = ad* <L. "to," "toward"]
tr. v. 1. To make slender or small.

Famine had **attenuated** the population of the village to a few dozen people.

2. To weaken; to reduce in force or value.

The forest of tall trees **attenuated** the force of the gale before it hit the town.

6. **tenuous**   (tĕn′yōō əs)
adj. 1. Thin in form.

The spider spun a web of **tenuous** threads.

2. Flimsy; having little substance or validity.

Most students have only a **tenuous** grasp of economics.

tenuously, *adv.*

Familiar Words
asset
satisfaction
satisfy

SATIS <L. "enough"

7. satiate (sā′shē āt)
tr. v. To satisfy an appetite fully; to gratify to excess.

During our stay in Italy we **satiated** ourselves on art, opera, and pasta.

satiation, *n.*; **satiety** (sə tī′ĭ tē), *n.*

Familiar Words
accomplish
complete
plenty
replenish
supply

IMPLEO, IMPLERE, IMPLEVI, IMPLETUM <L. "to fill"
PLENUS <L. "full"

Challenge Words
plenary
plenipotenitary
plenitude
plenum

8. comply (kəm plī′) [*com = cum* <L. intensifier]
intr. v. To do as one is asked or ordered.

Many historians believe the civil rights movement began in earnest when Rosa Parks refused to **comply** with the law requiring black people to sit in the back of the bus.

compliance, *n.*; **compliant**, *adj.*; **compliancy**, *n.*

9. implement (ĭm′plə mənt) [*im = in* <L. intensifier]
n. A tool or utensil.

Inventor Cyrus McCormick's **implement** for harvesting grain, the "McCormick reaper," revolutionized nineteenth-century agriculture.

tr. v. To carry out; to put into effect.

Using old newspapers and yearbooks, we were able to **implement** our project to trace the history of our school.

10. replete (rĭ plēt′) [*re* <L. "again"]
adj. 1. Well-stocked or abundantly supplied.

I like a novel **replete** with suspense and danger.

2. Completely filled; utterly satisfied.

Replete with Thanksgiving dinner, we agreed to postpone doing the dishes.

repletion, *n.*; **repletely**, *adv.*

11. expletive (ĕk'splĭ tĭv) [*ex* <L. "out"]
n. An exclamation or oath, often obscene.

Although we couldn't speak their language, we could tell they were uttering angry **expletives** at us.

expletory, *adj.*

EXERCISE 5A Circle the letter of the best SYNONYM (the word or phrase most nearly the same as the word in bold-faced type).

1. to **satiate** one's hunger   a. vaunt   b. satisfy   c. lessen   d. fail to satisfy   e. duplicate
2. regard as a **microcosm**   a. substitute   b. reduced version   c. distortion   d. vacuity   e. minor problem
3. to **implement** a plan   a. enlarge   b. carry out   c. form   d. criticize   e. negate
4. utter a loud **expletive**   a. insult   b. belch   c. monologue   d. exclamation   e. refusal
5. inhabited by primitive **microbes**   a. insects   b. recluses   c. microcosms   d. humans   e. organisms

Circle the letter of the best ANTONYM (the word or phrase most nearly opposite the word in bold-faced type).

6. to feel **replete**   a. satiated   b. sentimental   c. empty   d. regretful   e. reclusive
7. a(n) **minuscule** portion   a. tasteful   b. enormous   c. unilateral   d. thrifty   e. delicious
8. a **tenuous** friendship   a. new   b. totalitarian   c. firm   d. weak   e. sensitive
9. a(n) **compliant** nature   a. obedient   b. lazy   c. rebellious   d. frightened   e. catholic
10. concerned with **minutiae**   a. oneself   b. petty facts   c. time   d. nihilism   e. large concepts

EXERCISE 5B Circle the letter of the sentence in which the word in bold-faced type is used incorrectly.

1. a. **Minuscule** particles of frost reflected the sun's light.
   b. Only a **miniscule** proportion of students today studies Greek.
   c. Rural Americans often attended a one-room **miniscule**.
   d. This film can detect even a **minuscule** ray of light.

2. a. The starving dog had become so **attenuated** that its collar slipped off.
   b. Although **attenuated** by fasting, Mahatma Gandhi remained influential in India's struggle for independence from the British.
   c. Bombing raids failed to **attenuate** symphony audiences in London during "the Blitz" of World War II.
   d. Your library fines will be **attenuated** from your allowance.

3. a. I've never known them to be so **replete** that they turned down a second helping.
   b. We returned from camp **replete** with memories.
   c. Since I lost Volume 12, my encyclopedia is no longer **replete**.
   d. The National Gallery in Washington, D.C., is **replete** with American art from all periods.

4. a. Despite her fatigue, **tenuous** determination drove her to finish the race.
   b. She offered only a **tenuous** reason for her tardiness.
   c. Only a **tenuous** strand of rope held the boat to its mooring.
   d. Despite a **tenuous** grasp of Arabic, we managed to follow the villagers' directions.

5. a. **Comply** the sheets carefully when they are dry.
   b. His **compliant** nature made him easy to bully.
   c. In **compliance** with Thai etiquette, we carefully avoided turning our feet toward our hosts.
   d. Although she found the contest rules unusual, she knew she had to **comply** with them to win the prize.

6. a. Our principal has begun to **implement** the school board's new conservation program by installing paper recycling bins in every classroom.
   b. Until the invention of the fork in the sixteenth century, the only eating **implement** most Europeans used was a knife.
   c. Your bike is **implementing** the driveway again!
   d. Once the law setting the speed limit at 55 miles per hour was **implemented**, traffic deaths dropped markedly.

EXERCISE 5C   Fill in each blank with the most appropriate word from Lesson 5. Use a word or any of its forms only once.

1. A family group can be regarded as a _____ of all human relations.

2. The angry customer yelled an _____ at the stunned cashier.

3. Forecasters expect the force of the hurricane to _____ as it moves inland and loses most of its moisture.

4. Until the invention of the microscope made them visible, the existence of _____s was unknown.

5. Some teachers seem more concerned with the _____ of writing—whether an *i* is dotted or a *t* is crossed—than with what students have to say.

6. After turkey and all the trimmings, we were too _____d to eat any pumpkin pie.

LESSON 6

Magna est veritas et praevalet.
The truth is great and it will prevail.—ESDRAS

Key Words		
copious	magnate	megalomania
macrocosm	magnitude	polygamy
magnanimous		polygon

Familiar Word
copy

Challenge Word
cornucopia

COPIA <L. "plenty"

1. **copious**   (kō′pē əs)
   adj. Plentiful; in large amounts.

   The **copious** correspondence of Madame de Sévigné written to her daughter gives a vivid picture of her life in the court of Louis XIV.

   copiously, *adv.*

Challenge Words
macrobiotic
macroscopic
macrostructure

MAKROS <G. "large"

2. **macrocosm**   (măk′rə kŏz´əm)   [*kosmos* <G. "universe"]
   n. 1. The universe.

   Theoretical physicists have attempted to determine the size of the **macrocosm**.

   2. Any great whole.

Try to imagine your own family in relation to the **macrocosm** of the human family.

macrocosmic, *adj.*
Antonym: **microcosm**

MAGNUS <L. "great"

3. magnanimous (măg nắn′ə məs) [*animus* <L. "mind," "spirit"]
adj. Noble and generous, especially in forgiving; not petty.

On her deathbed she made the **magnanimous** gesture of forgiving all debts owed her.

magnanimity, *n.*; **magnanimously**, *adv.*

4. magnate (măg′nāt, măg′nĭt)
n. A wealthy, influential person, especially in business.

Ezra Cornell, a lumber **magnate**, left his fortune to found Cornell University.

5. magnitude (măg′nĭ tōōd, măg′nĭ tyōōd)
n. 1. Greatness of importance or size.

Early explorers of the South American coast had no idea of the **magnitude** of the continent.

2. The degree of brightness of a star.

The constellation Orion contains two stars of the highest **magnitude**, Betelgeuse and Rigel.

MEGAS <G. "great"

6. megalomania (mĕg′ə lō mān′ē ə, mĕg′ə lō mān′yə) [*mania* <G. "madness"]
n. 1. A form of mental illness in which a person has exaggerated ideas of his or her own importance.

His **megalomania** prevents him from recognizing his faults or appreciating the talents of others.

2. An obsessive idea to do things on a grand scale.

Megalomania drove the couple to build a swimming pool larger than their modest house.

megalomaniac, *n.*

NOTA BENE: Both of the prefixes *demi* and *semi* indicate "half" or "partial." *Demi* usually means "less than full size or status" as in *demitasse*, a small cup. *Semi* means "part," as in *semiformal, semiofficial, semifinal*, or *semiprecious*, or it can indicate "half" as in *semicircle* or *semiannual*.

Challenge Words
polyglot
polygraph
polynomial
polyphonic
polysyllabic
polytechnic

POLY <G. "many"

7. **polygamy** (pə lĭg′ə mē) [*gamos* <G. "marriage"]
n. The system of having more than one spouse at a time.

Although **polygamy** was not generally practiced in ancient Greece, the rulers were allowed to be polygamous to guarantee that they would have heirs.

polygamous, *adj.*; **polygamously**, *adv.*

8. **polygon** (pŏl′ē gŏn) [*gonia* <G. "angle"]
n. A flat shape with many straight sides.

Each of the five-pointed stars on the American flag is a **polygon**.

polygonal, *adj.*; **polygonally**, *adv.*

EXERCISE 6A

Circle the letter of the best SYNONYM (the word or phrase most nearly the same as the word in bold-faced type).

1. underestimate their **magnitude**   a. weight   b. strength   c. fame
   d. generosity   e. great importance
2. a(n) **polygonal** shape   a. many-sided   b. pretty   c. bipartisan
   d. attractive   e. tenuous
3. to study **polygamy**   a. the practice of having many wives   b. the
   environment   c. many-legged creatures   d. the effects of learning
   many languages   e. the interaction of many cultures

Circle the letter of the best ANTONYM (the word or phrase most nearly opposite the word in bold-faced type).

4. become a(n) **magnate**   a. beggar   b. attraction   c. aristocrat
   d. invalid   e. recluse
5. receive **copious** praise   a. eloquent   b. minuscule   c. long-winded
   d. catholic   e. omniscient
6. a(n) **magnanimous** offer   a. selfish   b. excessively proud
   c. sweeping   d. unilateral   e. overt
7. unmistakable **megalomania**   a. modesty   b. vacuity   c. reclusiveness
   d. vanity   e. madness

EXERCISE 6B   Circle the letter of the sentence in which the word in bold-faced type is used incorrectly.

1. a. Only a **megalomaniac** would build a fifty-room mansion in the middle of the desert.
   b. Her **megalomania** became so acute that she considered running for president.
   c. The executive's **megalomania** was intensified by his popular success.
   d. Could **megalomania** result from trying to overcome deep-seated feelings of inferiority?

2. a. Although his brothers had once deeply hurt his feelings, Joseph **magnanimously** forgave them.
   b. Her **magnanimous** criticism wounded him deeply.
   c. Lincoln urged the North to show **magnanimity** to the defeated South, "with malice toward none and charity toward all."
   d. My parents **magnanimously** let me borrow their new car, despite the dents I had put in the old one.

3. a. Physicists believe the **macrocosm** to be expanding rapidly.
   b. To understand global weather patterns, meteorologists must consider the earth as a **macrocosm**, with all nations interdependent.
   c. Any neighborhood can serve as a **macrocosm** for the society as a whole.
   d. The laws of science are thought to be **macrocosmic** in their application; we expect light to travel at the same speed in any galaxy.

4. a. The **magnitude** of earthquakes is measured on the Richter scale, with a 1 representing a minor rumble and anything over 7 a major disaster.
   b. We greatly appreciate your **magnitude** in making this generous donation.
   c. The Nobel Prize in literature goes to a writer who has created works of the highest **magnitude**.
   d. The twenty brightest stars are classified as being "of the first **magnitude**."

EXERCISE 6C   Fill in each blank with the most appropriate word from Lesson 6. Use a word or any of its forms only once.

1. At its height the empire of William Randolph Hearst, the newspaper _____, included more than 100 publications.

2. In some _____ societies the greater the number of wives, the greater is a man's social status.

3. A _____ can have as few as three sides or as many as can be calculated.

4. Drink _____ amounts of water when you have a fever.

5. Modern science has led us to see the _____ as a vast interrelated system of forces.

6. Their _____ drove them to buy a limousine, though they could not even afford repairs or gasoline, much less a chauffeur.

7. The new prime minister _____ly appointed her political opponents to join in the new administration.

REVIEW EXERCISES FOR LESSONS 5 AND 6

1 Fill in the blank or circle the letter of the best answer.

1. *mikros* : *makros* ::
   a. big : little
   b. *minuere* : *implere*
   c. *satis* : enough
   d. *plenus* : empty
   e. microcosm : macrocosm
2. *mono* : *poly* ::
   a. many : one
   b. monopoly : game
   c. polygon : monogram
   d. 1 : 0
   e. one : many
3. *Attenuate* and *tenuous* come from the Latin root _____,

   which means to _____ .
4. *Copious* comes from the Latin root *copia*, which means _____ .
5. Both the Latin root _____ and the Greek root _____
   mean "great".

2 Writing or Discussion Activities

1. Some school courses require learning a great deal of *minutiae*.
   Describe such a course using *minutia* or *minutiae* in your sentence.
2. Write two sentences that show the different meanings of *attenuate*.
   Use *attenuate* in both sentences.
3. Revise and improve these sentences. Try to reduce the number of
   words, especially those in italics.
   a. The *powerful business leaders* uttered *obscene exclamations* when they
      found out that their monopoly of the steel industry had become
      flimsy and unsubstantial.
   b. What seem to be *unimportant details* can yield *plentiful* information
      to a skillful detective.
   c. Although a drop of water may seem *extremely small* to the naked
      eye, under a microscope it appears a *miniature world* teeming with
      different life forms.
4. Describe a *magnanimous* act made by someone you have known. Use
   magnanimous or *magnanimity* in your sentence.

LESSONS 7 AND 8

Before and After

LESSON 7

Praemonitus, praemunitus.
Forewarned is forearmed.

Key Words		
antebellum	precept	premonition
antecedent	predestination	preposterous
anterior	preempt	pretentious
avant-garde		vanguard

Familiar Words
advance
ancient

ANTE <L. "before"

1. **antebellum** (ăn´tē bĕl´əm)   [*bellum* <L. "war"]
    adj. Of a period before a war, especially the American Civil War.

    Gone with the Wind describes life in **antebellum** Georgia.

2. **antecedent** (ăn´tə sēd´ənt)   [*cedere* <L. "to go"]
    n. 1. A thing or event that precedes.

    The Anglo-Saxon word *hlaf*, meaning "bread," is the **antecedent** of the modern word *loaf*.

Challenge Words
ante
antedate
antediluvian
ante meridiem
anteroom

2. (grammar) The noun to which a pronoun refers.

In "She took a book and read it," *book* is the **antecedent** of *it*.

adj. Preceding; going before.

Writing the final paper was **antecedent** to his passing the class.

antecede, *v.*; **antecedently**, *adv.*

3. **anterior**   (ăn tîr′ē ər)
adj. Coming before in position or time.

The aquatic larval stage of a tadpole is **anterior** to the full-grown state of a frog.

anteriorly, *adv.*

4. **avant-garde**   (ä′vänt gärd)
adj. Ahead of the times, especially in the arts.

Although considered extremely **avant-garde** in the nineteenth century, Impressionist paintings are now so popular that they appear on calendars and greeting cards.

n. A group that is ahead of the times.

Fashions worn only by the **avant-garde** are seen everywhere after a few years.

5. **vanguard**   (văn′gärd)   [short for French *avant garde*]
n. 1. The foremost position, especially of an army or fleet.

At Agincourt, English archers decimated the French **vanguard** of mounted knights in armor.

2. Leaders of a movement, fashion, etc.

The **vanguard** of the French Revolution discarded their powdered wigs and wore their hair naturally.

Familiar Words
precaution
precede
predict
prefix
premium
preoccupied
prepare
preposition
prescribe
preside
presume
pretend
prevail
prevent

Challenge Words
preamble
precinct
precipitate
précis
precocious
preconceive
preeminent
premise
preponderant
prerequisite
prerogative
prescience
prevalent
prevaricate

PRE <L. "before"

6. precept (prē′sĕpt) [*capere* <L. "to take"]
n. A command; a rule of conduct.

Although his parents tried to teach him the **precepts** of good manners, he remained tactless and inconsiderate.

preceptive, *adj.*

7. predestination (prē dĕs′tə nā′shən) [*destinare* <L. "to determine"]
n. The belief that what happens in human life has already been determined by some higher power.

The couple felt that **predestination** had brought them together.

predestinate, *v.*; **predestine**, *v.*; **predestined**, *adj.*

8. preempt, pre-empt (prē ĕmpt′) [*emere* <L. "to buy"]
tr. v. To take possession of something before anyone else can do so.

The president's address **preempted** regular broadcasts.

preemption, *n.*; **preemptive**, *adj.*

9. premonition (prē mə nĭsh′ən, prĕm′ə nĭsh′ən) [*monere* <L. "to warn"]
n. A warning in advance.

As she picked up the letter, she had a **premonition** that it carried bad news.

premonitory, *adj.*

10. preposterous (prĭ pŏs′tər əs) [*post* <L. "after"]
adj. Absurd; contrary to nature or reason.

The long skirts and high collars of the nineteenth century seem **preposterous** to active modern women.

preposterously, *adv.*; **preposterousness**, *n.*

11. pretentious (prĭ tĕn′shəs) [*tendere* <L. "to extend"]
adj. Showy; pompous; claiming unjustified distinction.

They chose a hotel with **pretentious** furnishings but little comfort.

pretension, *n.*; **pretentiously**, *adv.*; **pretentiousness**, *n.*

EXERCISE 7A   Circle the letter of the best SYNONYM (the word or phrase most nearly the same as the word in bold-faced type).

1. a(n) **antebellum** attitude   a. anti-war   b. preclusive   c. pro-war
   d. pre-war   e. Southern
2. a(n) **anterior** position   a. forward   b. rear   c. side   d. awkward
   e. inside
3. in the **vanguard** of technology   a. forefront   b. aftermath
   c. business   d. protection   e. interest

Circle the letter of the best ANTONYM (the word or phrase most nearly opposite the word in bold-faced type).

4. a(n) **preposterous** idea   a. stubborn   b. silly   c. original
   d. reasonable   e. vacuous
5. a(n) **avant-garde** film   a. popular   b. dull   c. tenuous
   d. G-rated   e. out-of-date
6. wore a(n) **pretentious** outfit   a. attenuated   b. homemade
   c. out-of-style   d. miniscule   e. modest

EXERCISE 7B   Circle the letter of the sentence in which the word in bold-faced type is used incorrectly.

1. a. We resented the faculty's **preemption** of the new library books
      before we students ever got to see them.
   b. The Great Depression had **preempted** his hopes for college.
   c. **Preempt** the bottles before returning them for deposit.
   d. All the 50-yard-line seats had been **preempted** months ago by
      season ticket holders.
2. a. All new trucks have a steel **vanguard** to prevent theft.
   b. The English sighted the **vanguard** of the Armada off the Dover
      coast.
   c. Frank Lloyd Wright led the **vanguard** of early twentieth-century
      architecture.
   d. Because it enters an area first, a platoon's **vanguard** is frequently
      ambushed in jungle warfare.
3. a. A good teacher is always **preceptive** about whether or not
      students are paying attention.
   b. One important **precept** of Chinese culture is respect for elders.
   c. Nineteenth-century textbooks were **preceptive**, containing stories
      to illustrate good behavior.
   d. According to the **precepts** of the Buddha, all forms of life should
      be respected.

4. a. Don't be **preposterous**! You can't catch warts from handling a toad.
    b. Youth is no excuse for **preposterousness**.
    c. Because we arrived at the party **preposterously**, we had to wait around for things to get started.
    d. Until the 1970s most Olympic officials considered including a women's marathon to be a **preposterous** idea.

5. a. On the night before Julius Caesar's assassination, his wife had a **premonitory** dream that evil would befall her husband.
    b. In the Middle Ages comets and eclipses of the sun or moon were considered to be **premonitory** of the fall of kings.
    c. I had a **premonition** that you would call today!
    d. She resigned her position without giving any **premonition** for her action.

6. a. The larva and cocoon stages **antecede** the mature development of a moth.
    b. The **antecedent** of *they, them,* and *their* must be a plural noun.
    c. September is **antecedent** to December.
    d. Don't **antecede** between me and the light when I'm trying to read.

EXERCISE 7C   Fill in each blank with the most appropriate word from Lesson 7. Use a word or any of its forms only once.

1. Believers in astrology consider the sign under which one is born to

    _____ one to certain personality traits.

2. Many people think that a dream can contain a _____ of evil to come.

3. The economy of _____ Virginia depended on agriculture, but since the Civil War industry has been developed.

4. As Laertes departs for the university, his father Polonious reminds him of the many _____s that should guide his behavior.

5. A blow to the forehead could damage the _____ part of the brain.

6. Styles that seem _____ when they first appear often become old-fashioned in a few years.

7. Although they lived in debtors' prison, the Dorrit family made _____ references to their distinguished background and snubbed other inmates as their social inferiors.

8. To understand the significance of a major historical event like the American Revolution, you need to understand its _____ s and its consequences.

9. When I reached the park, I found all the camp sites had been _____ ed by a bird-watchers' convention.

LESSON 8

Primus inter pares.
The first among equals.

Key Words		
premier	primeval	posterior
primate	primordial	posterity
prime		posthumous

Familiar Words
primary
prime minister
prime number
prime time
primer
primitive
primrose

Challenge Words
prima donna
prima facie
primal
prime meridian
primogeniture

PRIMUS <L. "first"

1. **premier**   (prē′mē ər, prĕm′ē ər, prĭ mîr′)
adj. First in time or importance.

The winners of the Super Bowl are considered the **premier** football team in the nation.

n. A prime minister or head of state.

Golda Meir sought peace for Israel during her tenure as **premier**.

premiership, *n.*

NOTA BENE: Don't confuse *premier* with *premiere*, which derives from the same root but means either the first public performance of something (". . . the American *premiere*) or the female star of a theatrical company (She is the *premiere* of the Bolshoi Ballet).

2. **primate**   (prī′mĭt, prī′māt)
n. 1. An archbishop or bishop who ranks highest among others.

The Archbishop of Canterbury is **primate** of England.

2. A member of the order of animals that includes monkeys, apes, and humans.

All **primates** have large-sized brains.

3. **prime** (prīm)

    n. First in rank, excellence, quality, importance, or time.

    People disagree about which stage represents the **prime** of life.

    adj. Chief; most important.

    Television networks schedule their best programs during **prime** time, when the greatest number of people are watching.

    tr. v. To prepare something or someone for use or action.

    The coach's pregame talk **primed** the team to play hard.

4. **primeval** (prī mē′vəl) [*aevum* <L. "age"]
    adj. Belonging to the first ages; ancient.

    A **primeval** lake once covered most of California's San Joaquin Valley.

    primevally, *adv.*

5. **primordial** (prī môr′dē əl) [*ordiri* <L "to begin"]
    adj. Primeval; original; fundamental.

    Human beings have a **primordial** instinct for survival.

    primordially, *adv.*

POST <L. "after"

6. **posterior** (pŏ stîr′ē ər, pō stîr ē ər)
    adj. Situated behind or at the back.

    Many automobiles in the 1920s and 1930s had a "rumble seat," an extra, **posterior** seat that opened out from what we now call the trunk.

    posteriorly, *adv.*
    Antonym: **anterior**

7. **posterity** (pŏ stĕr′ə tē)
    n. 1. Future generations.

    Will our **posterity** inherit any wilderness lands at all?

2. A person's descendants.

The maker of this lace tablecloth would be glad to know that four generations of her **posterity** have continued to use it.

8. **posthumous** (pŏs′cho͞o məs) [*humus* <L. "earth"]
adj. Occurring or continuing after death, especially a work published after the author's death or a child born after the father's death.

The Diary of Anne Frank, which recounts the young girl's experiences in the Holocaust, has brought Anne **posthumous** fame.

posthumously, *adv.*

NOTA BENE: You have been using *ante* and *post* most of your life, perhaps without knowing it. The abbreviations A.M. and P.M. to indicate times before and after noon stand for *ante meridiem*, "before noon," and *post meridiem*, "after noon."

EXERCISE 8A

Circle the letter of the best SYNONYM (the word or phrase most nearly the same as the word in bold-faced type).

1. a(n) **primordial** stage a. principal b. omnipotent c. monolithic
   d. primeval e. developing
2. the **premier** athlete a. incipient b. prime c. vaunted d. famous
   e. omnipresent
3. leave to **posterity** a. one's offspring b. one's own choice
   c. chance d. the vanguard e. uncertainty

Circle the letter of the best ANTONYM (the word or phrase most nearly opposite the word in bold-faced type).

4. a(n) **prime** witness a. immature b. insignificant c. magnanimous
   d. rare e. avant-garde
5. a(n) **primeval** event a. civilized b. irrational c. artistic
   d. primordial e. contemporary
6. a(n) **posterior** position a. frontal b. squatting c. bilateral
   d. upright e. courageous

EXERCISE 8B

Circle the letter of the sentence in which the word in bold-faced type is used incorrectly.

1. a. Charles Darwin regarded humans as highly developed **primates**.
   b. The **primate** of the Episcopal Church is elected by the council of bishops.

    c. Babe Ruth set the **primate** record for home runs in a single season.

    d. **Primates** have a highly social nature.

  2. a. Many males of Queen Victoria's **posterity** were hemophiliacs.

    b. We must preserve natural resources for our nation's **posterity**.

    c. Looking into **posterity**, I remember my school days as though they were yesterday.

    d. What will **posterity** think about twentieth-century glass skyscrapers?

  3. a. The war correspondent's story of the invasion appeared **posthumously**, for she herself was killed in the battle.

    b. Gerald Manley Hopkins requested that most of his poetry be published **posthumously** because he felt it conflicted with his priestly duties.

    c. I was a **posthumous** child, born two months after my father's death.

    d. Despite their **posthumous** confessions, the accused were burned at the stake.

  4. a. Our **prime** purpose in Mexico was to study Spanish, but we also made many friends.

    b. Although she only swims laps today, in her **prime** my grandmother was an Olympic diver.

    c. If you weren't so **prime**, you'd have more fun.

    d. Eerie music **primed** the audience to expect that something frightening was about to happen.

  5. a. Henry Wadsworth Longfellow's poem *Evangeline* describes the "forest **primeval**" that covered America before European settlement.

    b. Many people consider environmental pollution to be the **primeval** of our time.

    c. Eohippus, a **primeval** horse about the size of a collie, was the prey of huge, flesh-eating dinosaurs.

    d. The Yosemite Valley was formed by **primeval** glaciers that cut a deep chasm through a once-gentle river bed.

EXERCISE 8C

Fill in each blank with the most appropriate word from Lesson 8. Use a word or any of its forms only once.

1. On a "bicycle built for two," or tandem bike, one cyclist sits

_____ to the other.

2. Do you think that our _____ will continue to eat the same kinds of food and live in the same kinds of houses as we do today?

3. Although he died an unknown pauper, Edgar Allan Poe has

   achieved _____ recognition.

4. Gorillas are the largest of the _____s.

5. The teacher tried to _____ the class for the
   examination by giving them practice exercises.

6. The _____s of the Common Market countries
   met to discuss the Parliament of Europe.

REVIEW EXERCISES FOR LESSONS 7 AND 8

1   Fill in the blank or circle the letter of the best answer.

1. The words *primary, prime minister,* and *primitive* derive from the root

    _____ , which means _____ .

2. The Latin words _____ and _____ both mean
    "before."

3. Explain how the meaning of *primus* relates to these words.

    a. a primer: _____

    b. primary school: _____

    c. the verb *prime*: _____

4. primeval : primordial ::
    a. precept : concept
    b. pretended : pretentious
    c. precede : proceed
    d. antecede : precede
    e. *primus* : last

5. posterior : anterior ::
    a. A.M. : P.M.
    b. rearguard : vanguard
    c. front : back
    d. preposterous : outrageous
    e. incipient : completed

2   Writing or Discussion Activities

1. Have you ever had the experience of being preempted? Have you
    ever done any preempting yourself? In a brief paragraph describe
    the situation in which preemption occurred.

2. Write a sentence or two in which you give an example from your
    own experience, if possible, of a *premonition* that proved to be true.
    Use *premonition* or *premonitory* in your writing.

3. Write sentences in which you use any two words from the following
    groups.
    a. precept, primeval, primate
    b. pretentious, avant-garde, preposterous

4. Write a brief paragraph in which you describe how a person in the
    vanguard of today's fashions might dress. Use *vanguard* or *avant-
    garde* in your sentence.

PART TWO

Enjoying

Creativity

Directions

1. Determine how the Latin or Greek root is related in meaning and spelling to each defined—KEY—word that follows it.
2. Learn the pronunciation and definition(s) of each KEY word, and notice how the words are used in sentences.
3. Practice using the varied forms of KEY words.
4. Build your knowledge with all the information given: Latin mottoes, Familiar Words, Challenge Words, and Nota Bene references.
5. Complete the exercises.

LESSON 9

Ars longa, vita brevis.
Art is long; life is short.—HIPPOCRATES

Key Words		
artifact	depict	parody
artifice	incantation	pictograph
artisan	ode	recant
artless		rhapsody

ARS, ARTIS <L. "art"

1. **artifact**   (är′tə făkt)   [*facere* <L. "to make"]
   n. An object made by human beings; often refers to a primitive tool or other relic from an earlier period.

   In some distant future hula hoops and skateboards may become treasured **artifacts**.

2. **artifice**   (är′tə fĭs)   [*-fice = ficere* or *facere* <L. "to make"]
   n. 1. Craftiness; trickery.

   In the fable about a crow and a pitcher, the crow's **artifice** enables it to quench its thirst: it drops pebbles into the pitcher to raise the water level high enough to drink.

   2. Cleverness; skill.

   Dressing stylishly on a limited budget requires planning, imagination, and artifice.

   artificer, *n.*

3. **artless**   (ärt′lĭs)
   adj. 1. Without deceit or cunning; natural; simple.

   Because Miranda, Prospero's daughter in Shakespeare's *The Tempest*, has lived all her life on a remote island, she is **artless** in the ways of the world.

   2. Crude; ignorant; uncultured.

   The **artless** patrons at the movie theater left their trash on the floor by their seats.

   artlessness, *n.*
   Antonym: **artful**

4. **artisan**   (är′tə zăn, är′tə săn)
   n. A skilled craftsperson.

   George Hepplewhite was such a superb **artisan** that his furniture is still prized more than two centuries later.

Familiar Words
comedy
melody
tragedy

Challenge Words
hymnody
monody
prosody

AOIDE <G. "song"

5. ode   (ōd)
n. A poem usually addressed to a particular person, object or event that has stimulated deep and noble feelings in the poet.

Beginning his **ode** with the line, "O wild West Wind, thou breath of Autumn's being," Percy Bysshe Shelley expresses admiration for the wind's swiftness and power and asks it to scatter the poet's words "among mankind."

NOTA BENE: Appearing first in Greece, the ode has traditionally been a long poem written on the occasion of a national celebration or heroic feat. In more recent times it often conveys the poet's thoughts on a subject such as immortality or solitude; famous English writers of odes in the late eighteenth and early nineteenth centuries are Thomas Gray, William Wordsworth, Percy Bysshe Shelley, and John Keats. However, a poet may use the form to create a somewhat less serious effect, as do Gray in "Ode on the Death of a Favourite Cat Drowned in a Tub of Gold Fishes" and Robert Burns in "To a Mouse."

6. parody   (păr′ə dē)   [*para* <G. "alongside"]
n. A humorous imitation of a piece of literature or music.

Ogden Nash's **parody** of Joyce Kilmer's "Trees" bemoans the ugliness of billboards in a humorous way:

> I think that I shall never see
> A billboard lovely as a tree.
> Indeed, unless the billboards fall
> I'll never see a tree at all.

tr. v. To mimic a style, plot, or idea for comic effect.

Cartoonists sometimes **parody** contemporary political figures or events.

parodist, *n.*

NOTA BENE: The following is a parody of "'Twas the Night before Christmas":

'Twas the day before graduation
   And all through the school
The seniors were laid back,
   Trying to be cool.

They passed all their classes
   By cramming like mad
In hopes that the prom
   Would be "awesome" and "rad."

(STEVE JUBB, "'Twas the Day before Graduation")

7. **rhapsody**   (răp′sə dē)   [*rhaptein* <G. "to string," "to stitch together"]
n. Speech or writing expressing great pleasure or enthusiasm.

Visitors to the Grand Canyon often recount their impressions in a **rhapsody** of detail.

rhapsodic, *adj.*; **rhapsodist**, *n.*; **rhapsodize**, *v.*

NOTA BENE: The word *rhapsody* can also refer to a musical composition of irregular form. An example is George Gershwin's "Rhapsody in Blue," which combines jazz and classical music.

NOTA BENE: Although some scholars are questioning the origin of the word *tragedy*, it is thought to have begun in ancient Greece as an ode sung in honor of Dionysus, god of wine, animal life, and vegetation. The prize for the performance was a young goat [*tragos* <G. "goat"]. These songs grew into longer productions and eventually into plays. Today the word *tragedy* applies to a dramatic or literary work having a major character who struggles with a moral problem that leads to severe disappointment, ruin, or death. *Comedy* [*komos* <G. "merrymaking" and *aiodes* <G. "singer"] also began as a song honoring Dionysus but in a procession at spring and harvest festivals. Today the word *comedy* refers to a play, motion picture, or other work that is humorous and ends happily.

Familiar Words chant enchant

CANTO, CANTARE, CANTAVI, CANTATUM <L. "to sing"

8. **incantation**   (ĭn kăn tā′shən)   [*in* <L. "in"]
n. The chanting or speaking of words seeming to have magical power or used to create a magical spell.

The **incantation**, "Open, Sesame!" spoken in an *Arabian Nights* tale, derives from the magical powers associated with the sesame plant.

Challenge Words cant cantata canto cantor chanteuse descant

9. **recant**   (rĭ kănt′)   [*re* <L. "back"]
tr. v. To take back a formal statement or belief previously made known.

Although Galileo was convinced that the earth moves around the sun, he **recanted** this belief when it brought open conflict with the Catholic church.

recantation, *n.*

| **Familiar Words** |
| paint |
| pictorial |
| picture |
| picturesque |
| pigment |

PINGO, PINGERE, PINXI, PICTUM
<L. "to paint," "to embroider"

10. depict (dĭ pĭkt´) [*de* <L. "from"]
tr. v. 1. To paint, draw, or express in a picture or sculpture.

The Bayeux Tapestry **depicts** the Battle of Hastings fought in 1066 between the Saxons and the Norman invaders.

2. To describe; to picture in words.

Jade Snow Wong **depicts** the life of a girl growing up in San Francisco's Chinatown in her autobiography, *Fifth Chinese Daughter.*

11. pictograph (pĭc´tə grăf, pĭc´tə gräf) [*graph* <L. "a sharp-pointed tool for writing on waxen tablets"]
n. A picture or drawing representing words or ideas.

Pictographs on the walls of palaces in Yucatan have given archaeologists clues to Mayan mythology.

pictographic, *adj.*

EXERCISE 9A   Circle the letter of the best SYNONYM (the word or phrase most nearly the same as the word in bold-faced type).

1. to **depict** a bullfight   a. paint   b. attend   c. speak out against   d. photograph   e. enjoy
2. to **recant** testimony in court   a. sing out   b. take back   c. agree with   d. repeat   e. disprove
3. the **artifice** of ancient Chinese painters   a. originality   b. lack of talent   c. imitation   d. skill   e. beauty
4. inspired by the **ode**   a. poem   b. story   c. strange writing   d. humorous verse   e. portrait
5. a skilled **artisan**   a. cartoonist   b. painter   c. craftsperson   d. storyteller   e. poet
6. praised the **artifact**   a. truthful statement   b. poem   c. skill   d. dishonest statement   e. relic
7. remembered the **incantation**   a. hieroglyphics   b. trick   c. magician   d. magic spell   e. description

Circle the letter of the best ANTONYM (the word or phrase most nearly the opposite word in bold-faced type).

8. annoyed by the **parody**   a. cartoon   b. imitation   c. lies
    d. serious, original work   e. lack of skill
9. a(n) **artless** young journalist   a. ignorant   b. simple
    c. unskilled   d. deceitful   e. inartistic
10. a(n) **rhapsodic** retelling of a movie plot   a. excited   b. long-
    winded   c. musical   d. poetic   e. unenthusiastic

EXERCISE 9B   Circle the letter of the sentence in which the word in bold-faced type is used incorrectly.

1. a. No amount of **incantation** persuaded my parents to let me see my graduation present before the day.
    b. The priestess uttered an **incantation** to summon the Greek goddess Artemis.
    c. As the fortune-teller murmured an **incantation**, we waited to learn our future.
    d. The three witches in *Macbeth* toss strange objects into the boiling pot, chanting an **incantation**: "Double, double toil and trouble;/ Fire burn, and cauldron bubble."
2. a. The athlete refused to **recant** his claim that he had never used steroids to give him an advantage over other athletes.
    b. The children **recanted** the song until they knew it by heart.
    c. Sometimes witnesses in court cases **recant** their earlier testimony, raising questions about what really happened.
    d. To try to save her life, Joan of Arc **recanted** her assertion that divine voices had guided her to become the savior of France.
3. a. Frankie Addams, an **artless** twelve-year-old in *A Member of the Wedding*, expects to accompany her brother and his wife on their honeymoon.
    b. The painter became restless when she had to remain **artless** during her long hospital treatment.
    c. Although **artless** in knowledge of manners at home and at school, Huckleberry Finn is instinctively wise in distinguishing good and evil in human beings.
    d. The **artless** smiles of babies are universally appealing.
4. a. Amateur detective Nancy Drew is notable for her **artifice** in finding clues.

b. Penelope promises to remarry when she completes her weaving but deceives her suitors by the **artifice** of unraveling it every night.

c. Through the **artifice** of disguise, Deborah Sampson was able to enlist as a private in the Revolutionary War.

d. The antique dealer displayed a collection of famous **artifices** in the shop window.

5. a. Egyptian **pictographs**, called *hieroglyphics*, show everyday tasks such as wheat and barley harvesting, weaving, and hunting.

b. Some characters used to write Chinese were originally **pictographic**, but now they are stylized representations of objects, figures, or symbols.

c. The sound recording we made during a whitewater rafting trip has become a treasured **pictograph**.

d. Many of the brands that Mexican herders used to identify horses and cattle were designs copied from Native American **pictographs**.

EXERCISE 9C   Fill in each blank with the most appropriate word from Lesson 9. Use a word or any of its forms only once.

1. The Toltecs of northern Mexico were master _____s who decorated palace walls with horizontal bands of mythological figures.

2. The American painter Mary Cassatt _____ed family scenes and intimate interiors.

3. "Casey at the Bat" is a familiar verse that lends itself well to comic imitations, or _____.

4. Arrowheads and pottery are two kinds of _____s that inform us about early Native American culture in the United States.

5. When expressing powerful feelings in a long, formal poem, or _____, poets have chosen such subjects as solitude, evening, and the west wind.

6. Detective Sherlock Holmes is always capable of _____ more subtle than that of the criminal he pursues.

7. _____s written on the rock walls of the cave help us imagine what life was like in primitive times.

LESSON 10

Facile princeps.
Easily the leader.

Key Words

accrue	efficacious	faction
beneficence	excrescence	mollify
context	facile	pretext
crescendo	facsimile	

Familiar Words
adolescence
concrete
crescent
crew
decrease
increase
recruit

Challenge Words
concrescence
convalescent
Creole
fluorescence
luminescence
opalescence
phosphorescence
senescence

CRESCO, CRESCERE, CREVI, CRETUM <L. "to grow," "to increase"

1. **accrue** (ə krōō′) [*ac* = *ad* <L. "to," "toward"]
intr. v. To come as a natural increase or advantage.

   Satisfaction **accrues** when people earn their living doing what they truly enjoy.

   accrual, *n.*

2. **crescendo** (krĭ shĕn′dō, krĭ sĕn′dō)
n. A gradual increase in sound, often referring to music.

   As the parade approached, the drum beat rose in a deafening **crescendo**.

   NOTA BENE: *Crescendo* can also be used as an adjective ("a *crescendo* effect") and an adverb ("the band played *crescendo*").

3. **excrescence** (ĕk skrĕs′əns) [*ex* <L. "from," "out of"]
n. Abnormal growth or outgrowth.

   Pictographs of mythological creatures often show **excrescences**: extra faces, arms, or legs.

   excrescent, *adj.*

   NOTA BENE: The familiar and challenge words with the suffix *-escent* or *-escence* derive from *crescere*, "to grow." They express the idea of growing: *adolescence, crescent, convalescent, fluorescence,* etc.

FACIO, FACERE, FECI, FACTUM <L. "to make"

4. **beneficence**   (bə něf′ə sěns)   [*bene* <L. "well," "good"]
n. Doing good or causing good to be done; kindly action.

The Peace Corps organizes many forms of American **beneficence** in countries throughout the world.

beneficient, *adj.*

5. **efficacious**   (ěf′ə kā′shəs)   [*ef* = *ex* <L. "from," "out of"]
adj. Effective as a means or remedy.

"Example is always more **efficacious** than precept."
—Samuel Johnson

efficaciously, *adv.*

6. **facile**   (fă′sĭl)
adj. Acting, working, or proceeding with ease; fluent. (Sometimes, superficial, when something is too easily done.)

Finalists in the national spelling bee are exceptionally **facile** spellers.

facilely, *adv.*; **facilitate**, *v.*; **facility**, *n.*

7. **facsimile**   (făk sĭm′ə lē)   [*simile* <L. "alike"]
n. An exact copy of a book, painting, document, etc.

Many libraries have a **facsimile** of the first printed edition of Shakespeare's plays.

NOTA BENE: *Facsimile* can also be used as an adjective, as in *facsimile* edition.

8. **faction**   (făk′shən)
n. 1. A group or clique within a larger group, party, or government.

In *Lord of the Flies* the society formed by the marooned schoolboys breaks into two **factions**, the hunters and the firebuilders.

2. Conflict within an organization or nation.

Because of heated faction on the location of missiles, Congress delayed a vote.

factional, *n.*; **factious**, *adj.*

9. **mollify** (mŏl′ə fī) [*mollis* <L. "soft"; *fy* = *ficare* or *facere* <L. "to make"]
tr. v. To calm; to make gentler or softer in feeling.

According to the fable, the goddess Juno cannot **mollify** the peacock, who frets because it lacks a pleasing voice to match its great beauty.

NOTA BENE: When you see the suffix *-fy* in a verb form, it probably comes from *facere* or *ficare*, both meaning "to make." The suffix appears in *amplify, deify, edify, justify, modify, notify,* and other words listed in this section.

As you can see, the Latin verb *facere* takes many forms in English words: *beatific, benefit, efficient, facility, defect, feature, forfeit,* and *feasible.*

TEXO, TEXERE, TEXUI, TEXTUM <L. "to weave"

10. **context** (kŏn′tĕkst) [*con* = *cum* <L. "with"]
n. 1. The parts before or after a word or statement that influence its meaning.

The **context** of "the *bow* of a ship" tells you that *bow* does not mean "a bending of the body" or "a weapon used with arrows."

2. The circumstances surrounding an event or situation.

In the **context** of World War II, the opening measures of Beethoven's Fifth Symphony became a message of hope to Nazi-occupied countries.

Familiar Words
text
textbook
textile
texture
tissue

Challenge Words
textual
textural

11. **pretext** (prē′tĕkst) [*pre* <L. "before"]
n. A false reason put forward to conceal the true one.

Using the **pretext** of a sore throat, I managed to stay home to see the whole World Series.

NOTA BENE: Closely linked to *texere* are the Latin verb *tego, tegere, texi, tectum,* "to cover," and the Greek noun *tekna,* "art," "craft." Words that derive from *tegere* include *architect, architecture, detect, polytechnic, protect, technicolor, technocracy,* and *toga.*

EXERCISE 10A   Circle the letter of the best SYNONYM (the word or phrase most nearly the same as the word in bold-faced type).

1. welcome **beneficence**   a. skill in a craft   b. kind thoughts
   c. good deeds   d. good looks   e. good fortune
2. an unconvincing **pretext**   a. introduction   b. explanation
   c. primer   d. first draft   e. excuse

Circle the letter of the best ANTONYM (the word or phrase most nearly opposite the word in bold-faced type).

3. a(n) **efficacious** remedy   a. efficient   b. imaginative   c. strong
   d. useless   e. powerful
4. to let good feelings **accrue**   a. decrease   b. gather   c. develop
   d. to be exchanged   e. to be wasted
5. a **facile** worker   a. skillful   b. clumsy   c. talkative   d. reluctant
   e friendly

EXERCISE 10B   Circle the letter of the sentence in which the word in bold-faced type is used incorrectly.

1. a. When we protested a program of all classical music, our band director **mollified** us with a Sousa march and some jazz.
   b. After coming in tardy, the freshmen tried to **mollify** their teacher by answering every question.
   c. The city council might have **mollified** skateboarders by voting for a skateboard park rather than prohibiting skateboarding altogether.
   d. We **mollified** the waffle batter by adding flour.
2. a. Advertisers try to convince use that one brand of aspirin is more **efficacious** than another.
   b. Spending twenty-four hours alone in the wilderness is **efficacious** in teaching self-reliance.
   c. The violinist bowed in response to the **efficacious** applause from the audience.
   d. In 1876 Lydia Pinkham offered to the public a mixture of roots, seeds, and alcohol that she claimed was "**efficacious**, immediate, and lasting" in curing a variety of disorders.
3. a. Although often entertaining, television interviews are too **facile** to be informative.
   b. The **facile** needles of quilt-makers have recorded family histories.
   c. Using a fishing rod with **facility** is my aim.
   d. People who can listen well are **facile** to talk to.

4. a. In Warsaw, Poland, **facsimiles** of buildings destroyed during
        World War II have been constructed.
    b. The **facsimile** features of the cousins were so striking that
        people thought they were twins.
    c. A special centennial edition of *The Hunting of the Snark* includes
        a complete **facsimile** of the first edition.
    d. A **facsimile** of a painting by Georgia O'Keeffe is worth much
        less than the original.

5. a. In the 1980s **faction** arose in the movie industry over the issue
        of adding color to classic movies originally filmed in black and
        white.
    b. One **faction** wants to celebrate Independence Day on July 4; the
        other prefers the nearest Monday.
    c. When a country engages in revising its history by concealing or
        altering facts, it commits **faction**.
    d. Although **faction** arose among planners of the Vietnam War
        Memorial, most visitors are moved by its design.

6. a. As the storm intensified, the **crescendo** of thunder made the
        house rattle.
    b. A gradual **crescendo** of voices at a party usually means that
        people are having a good time.
    c. The concerto ended with a rousing **crescendo** from the brass
        section of the orchestra.
    d. The tune played on the piano faded to a delicate **crescendo**.

7. a. Until the nineteenth century many people considered a
        mountain range a satanic **excrescence** rather than an example
        of natural beauty.
    b. Modern surgery provides remedies for people born with
        unsightly **excrescences** such as warts.
    c. The plane could not take off until the **excrescence** of baggage
        had been removed.
    d. Some mining companies are at fault for leaving ugly debris that
        is an **excrescence** on the landscape.

8. a. This book has a table of contents but no **pretext**.
    b. Presidential privilege may serve as a **pretext** for withholding
        information of public concern.
    c. In Homer's epic poem, *The Iliad,* the gift of a huge wooden
        horse is the **pretext** for sneaking Greek soldiers inside Troy.
    d. In the 1940s Germany justified invasions of neighboring
        countries on the **pretext** of needing more living space.

9. a. Abstract words like *beauty* and *justice* required a detailed **context** to have meaning.
    b. So many talented actors tried out for the school play that there weren't enough **contexts** to go around.
    c. When you read about the Middle Ages, put yourself into the **context** of the times.
    d. Sometimes newspaper reporters alter the meaning of public speakers by quoting them out of **context**.

REVIEW EXERCISES FOR LESSONS 9 AND 10

1 Circle the letter of the best answer to the following analogies.

1. *cantare* : to sing ::
    a. *facere* : to increase
    b. *texere* : to weave
    c. *pingere* : to carve
    d. *crescere* : to disappear
    e. *ars* : song
2. to destroy : *facere* ::
    a. *pingere* : to paint
    b. *aoide* : rhapsody
    c. to sing : *texere*
    d. to wither : *crescere*
    e. *texere* : to make
3. excrescence : grows ::
    a. recantation : chants
    b. facsimile : copies
    c. parody : honors
    d. beneficence : harms
    e. ode : warns
4. faction : agreement ::
    a. artlessness : worldliness
    b. accrual : increase
    c. poetry : ode
    d. artisan : craftsperson
    e. depiction : painting

5. Circle the letter of the pair that does *not* follow the pattern of the first pair.
   pretext : excuse ::
   a. artifact : handmade object
   b. facsimile : exact copy
   c. excrescence : normal growth
   d. rhapsody : enthusiastic description
   e. parody : humorous imitation

2 Writing or Discussion Activities

1. Improve these sentences by shortening them. Substitute words in this lesson for the words in italics and make any other changes needed for smoothness.
   a. Nothing could *help* the children *feel more cheerful* after the dog ate their birthday cake. (One word will take the place of four.)
   b. Butter used to be considered a remedy *that would work quickly and effectively* for burns, but now cold water is recommended.
   c. The magician uttered *words having magical powers.*
   d. They were so *ignorant of the ways of the world* that they thought their *false reason for doing something that they wanted to hide* would conceal their going to a movie.
   e. If you *take back what you have said earlier,* you need to have good reasons.

2. *Rhapsodize* about a recent experience. Show specific reasons for your intense pleasure or excitement, and use a form of *rhapsodize* in your writing.

3. Write a clear, lively sentence or two for each of the situations below, giving details to supply a specific context. Do NOT use any of the italicized words in your sentences; instead, let your details show your understanding of the words.
   a. Describe a *facile artisan.*
   b. Describe the *crescendo* of a piece of music that you know.
   c. Describe what happens when someone *mollifies* a *faction.*
   d. In what situation might someone *recant* a *parody*?

LESSONS 11 AND 12

Travel

LESSON 11

Sic transit gloria mundi.
Thus passes away the glory of this world.—THOMAS À KEMPIS

Key Words		
aberration	exodus	transient
ambience	obituary	transitive
episode	transgress	transitory
erratic		translucent

TRANS <L. "across"

1. **transgress**   (trăns grĕs′, trănz grĕs′)   [*gradi* <L. "to step"]
   tr. and *intr. v.* To go beyond or over set limits; to break
   a rule.

   According to the Bible, Adam and Eve **transgressed**
   God's command when they ate fruit from the tree of
   knowledge.

   transgression, *n.*

2. **transitive**   (trăn′sə tĭv, trăn′zə tĭv)   [*it* = *ire* <L. "to go"]
adj. (grammar) Describing an action carried from subject to verb to object; needing a direct object to complete the meaning of the verb.

The following sentence contains a **transitive** verb: "The tornado destroyed the town."

NOTA BENE: Some verbs can be both *transitive* (taking a direct object) and *intransitive* (not needing a direct object to complete the meaning). For example, in "The champion *broke* the record" *broke* is transitive and in "The glass *broke*" it is intransitive. Some verbs rarely, if ever, require a direct object: *lie* (meaning "to lie down"), *sleep*, and *die*. They are intransitive verbs.

3. **transitory**   (trăn′sĭ tōr′ē, trăn′sĭ tôr′ē)
[*it* = *ire* <L. "to go"]

adj. Lasting for only a short while.

In comedy, problems are **transitory**: misfortune ends and conflicts are resolved.

4. **translucent**   (trăns loo′sənt, trănz loo′sənt)   [*lucere* <L. "to shine"]
adj. Permitting light to pass through, but not transparent.

Sunlight through the **translucent** stained glass windows made colorful designs on the white walls.

translucence, *n.*; **translucently**, *adv.*

EO, IRE, IVI, ITUM <L. "to go"

5. **ambience** (ăm′bĭ əns) [*amb* <L. "on both sides"]
n. Environment; the surrounding atmosphere.

Many writers have described the **ambience** of Venice: its canals and gondolas, its squares and palaces.

ambient, *adj.*

6. **obituary**   (ō bĭch′oo ər′ē)   [*ob* <L. "because"]
n. Notice of a death with biographical information.

The **obituary** of Harriet Beecher Stowe included mention of her nine children and her novel *Uncle Tom's Cabin*.

7. **transient** (trăn′shənt, trăn′zhənt) [*trans* <L "across"]

adj. 1. Passing quickly; transitory.

Summer vacations are all too **transient**.

2. Staying only a short time.

Youth hostels cater to **transient** guests.

n. A person or thing having a short stay.

Canada geese are only **transients** in the Midwest, resting on their migration to the north.

transience, *n.*

ERRO, ERRARE, ERRAVI, ERRATUM <L. "to wander," "to stray"

8. **aberration** (ăb´ə rā′shən) [*ab* <L. "away from"]
n. Straying from what is normal or accepted.

Their fourth daughter became a lawyer, an **aberration** in this family of doctors.

aberrant, *adj.*

9. **erratic** (ĭ răt′ĭk)
adj. Irregular or inconsistent in movement, habit, quality, or ideas.

Because Alice meets so many strange characters like The Queen of Hearts and The Mad Hatter, her journey through Wonderland is highly **erratic**.

erratically, *adv.*

HODOS <G. "journey"

10. **episode** (ĕp′ə sōd) [*epi* <G. "upon," "to"]
n. An incident in a person's life or in a story or play.

The **episode** in *The Secret Garden* where lonely Mary Lennox discovers a hidden garden begins a story of friendship, believable magic, and the will to live.

episodic, *adj.*; **episodically**, *adv.*

11. **exodus** (ĕk′sə dəs) [*ex* <L. "from," "out of"]
n. 1. Mass departure or emigration.

The Spanish Civil War in the 1930s caused an **exodus** of refugees escaping to France.

2. (capitalized) The departure of the Israelites from Egypt with their leader Moses.

The second book of the Bible tells the story of the **Exodus** from Egypt to the promised land of Canaan.

EXERCISE 11A   Circle the letter of the best SYNONYM (the word or phrase most nearly the same as the word in bold-faced type).

1. a minor **transgression** a. sin b. omission c. change d. rebellion
   e. struggle
2. a(n) **aberration** in pulse rate   a. similarity   b. confusion
   c. abnormality   d. problem   e. consistency
3. a long **obituary** a. discussion   b. ode   c. death notice
   d. march   e. errand
4. an exciting **episode**   a. incident   b. biography   c. departure
   d. atmosphere   e. arrival

Circle the letter of the best ANTONYM (the word or phrase most nearly opposite the word in bold-faced type).

5. a forced **exodus** a. undertaking   b. emigration   c. entry
   d. announcement   e. excursion
6. a(n) **transient** at the hotel   a. permanent resident   b. employee
   c. diner   d. guest for a short stay   e. traveler
7. a gambler's **erratic** career   a. uneventful   b. orderly   c. irregular
   d. wandering   e. difficult
8. **transitory** memories   a. pleasant   b. sinful   c. fading   d. happy
   e. long-lasting

EXERCISE 11B   Circle the letter of the sentence in which the word in bold-faced type is used incorrectly.

1. a. The powerful spotlight made the bronze statue **translucent**.
   b. Until the **translucent** curtain, or scrim, rose, we could see the
      stage and actors only in dim outline.
   c. The **translucence** of the Tiffany lampshade lightens the room but
      protects the eyes.
   d. The muddy windshield was barely **translucent**.

2. a. Our holiday in Vancouver was too **transient** to let us see much of British Columbia.
    b. Fortunately for those allergic to pollen, the hay fever season is **transient**.
    c. The outmoded **transient** system was replaced by a monorail system.
    d. In the 1930s farmers in Oklahoma became **transients** when drought forced them off their land.

3. a. *Watership Down* depicts the **ambience** of the rabbit world as loyalties are tested and fears mount.
    b. Harlem in the 1920s offered an **ambience** stimulating to a group of American writers and performers.
    c. A quick **ambience** around the lake before dinner increased our appetites.
    d. Some travelers to Japan prefer the **ambience** of serene Kyoto to that of bustling Tokyo.

4. a. Now that they are playing in the finals, the soccer team can study only **erratically**.
    b. Nomadic people such as the Kashgai of Iran are **erratics** who have no permanent settlement.
    c. The **erratic** forces of wind shear and downdraft require quick responses from airline pilots.
    d. **Erratic** political forces have plagued South American countries.

EXERCISE 11C   Fill in each blank with the most appropriate word from Lesson 11. Use a word or any of its forms only once.

1. Mary Todd Lincoln's life was marked by three traumatic

    _____s: the deaths of sons Willie and Tad and the assassination of her husband, the president.

2. Most wildflowers are _____: they wilt soon after they are picked.

3. Years of drought in north central Africa have created a(n) _____ of refugees numbering in the thousands.

4. A _____ verb carries action from the doer to the receiver, as in "The batter smacked the ball."

5. Newspapers published a(n) _____ of Emperor Hirohito of Japan the day after his death in 1989.

6. In spite of its name, the French Quarter of New Orleans retains a

    Spanish colonial _____ from the years it belonged to Spain.

LESSON 12

Vade mecum.
Go with me.

Key Words		
advent	deviate	itinerant
circumvent	devious	itinerary
convene	impervious	telepathy
	intervene	

ITER, ITINERIS <L. "journey"

1. **itinerant**   (ī tĭn′ər ənt, ĭ tĭn′ər ənt)
adj. Traveling from place to place, especially to perform some duty or work; transient.

Johnny Appleseed led an **itinerant** life wandering through the Ohio Valley to give out apple seeds and saplings.

n. A person who travels from place to place.

Members of most herding tribes are **itinerants**, constantly on the move to find fresh grazing lands.

itinerancy, *n.*

2. **itinerary**   (ī tĭn′ə rĕr´ē, ĭ tĭn′ə rĕr´ē)
n. 1. A route of travel.

As interpreter and guide for the Lewis and Clark expedition, Sacajawea followed an **itinerary** that took her along the Missouri River, across the Rocky Mountains, to the Pacific Ocean.

2. A plan or record of a journey.

The team planning to climb Annapurna drew up a detailed **itinerary** of their route, base camps, and supply depots.

itinerate, *v.*

VENIO, VENIRE, VENI, VENTUM <L. "to come"

3. **advent**   (ăd'vĕnt)   [*ad* <L. "to"]
   n. 1. Arrival or coming into being.

   The change in foliage from green to red and yellow announces the **advent** of autumn.

   2. (capitalized) The period beginning four weeks before Christmas; the birth of Christ.

   During **Advent** Christians prepare to celebrate the birth of Christ.

4. **circumvent**   (sûr´kəm vĕnt')   [*circum* <L. "around"]
   tr. v. 1. To avoid; to evade by cleverness.

   Finding herself alone in a strange place, Viola in *Twelfth Night* **circumvents** discovery of her identity by disguising herself as a boy.

   2. To avoid by passing around.

   Freeways that **circumvent** cities ease traffic congestion downtown.

   circumvention, *n.*

5. **convene**   (kən vēn')   [*con = cum* <L. "with," "together with"]
   tr. and *intr. v.* To assemble, especially for a meeting.

   The First Continental Congress, which **convened** in 1774 in Philadelphia, Pennsylvania, began drafting the Declaration of Independence.

   convention, *n.*

6. **intervene**   (ĭn´tər vēn')   [*inter* <L. "between"]
   intr. v. 1. To occur between events or periods.

   One year **intervened** between the launching of the Soviet satellite *Sputnik* (1957) and the American satellite *Explorer* (1958).

   2. To come between, thereby easing a situation.

   Mary Poppins **intervenes** in the lives of the Banks children to make medicine palatable and adventures frequent.

   3. To interfere or to interrupt.

   In *Treasure Island* Long John Silver **intervenes** just as the young hero Jim devises ways to outwit him.

   intervention, *n.*

Familiar Words
telecast
telegram
telegraph
telephone
telephoto
telescope
television

TELE <G. "at a distance"

7. **telepathy** (tĕ lĕp'ə thē) [*pathos* <G. "passion," "suffering"]
n. Communication from one mind to another without speech, writing, or other sensory means.

Although a continent apart, the twins insisted that they could communicate through **telepathy**.

telepathic, *adj.*; **telepathically**, *adv.*

NOTA BENE: Although the Greek word *tele* has existed for thousands of years, most of its English derivatives have appeared since 1860, reflecting the surge of scientific and photographic inventions. Some are even more recent: *telegenic* means "possession of qualities appealing on television" and a telethon is a television broadcast soliciting support for a cause and lasting several hours.

Challenge Words
telegenic
telemeter
telethon
teletypist

Familiar Words
convey
obvious
previous
via
voyage

VIA <L. "way," "street," "road"; "journey"

8. **deviate** (dē'vē āt) [*de* <L. "away from"]
intr. v. To turn aside from a course, norm, pattern, or subject.

We try to get our English teacher to **deviate** from the lesson by asking about new books or movies.

deviant, *adj.* and *n.*; **deviation**, *n.*

Challenge Words
envoy
trivium
viaduct

9. **devious** (dē'vē əs) [*de* <L. "away from"]
adj. 1. Winding; roundabout.

In *Walkabout* an aboriginal leads home by a **devious** route two children lost in the Australian outback.

2. Underhanded; deceptive.

The two detectives, Miss Marple and Hercule Poirot, are quick to identify **devious** characters in Agatha Christie's mysteries.

deviousness, *n.*

10. **impervious** (ĭm pûr'vē əs) [*im = in* <L. "not"; *per* <L. "through"
adj. 1. Not penetrable by light rays, moisture, etc.

The new raincoats are **impervious** to water.

2. Incapable of being influenced or affected.

Florence Nightingale was **impervious** to her family's objections that a career in nursing was unladylike.

imperviousness, *n.*

EXERCISE 12A

Circle the letter of the best SYNONYM (the word or phrase most nearly the same as the word in bold-faced type).

1. a welcome **advent**   a. commercial   b. departure   c. arrival
   d. adventure   e. introduction
2. a weary **itinerant**   a. wanderer   b. travel agent   c. artisan   d. stay-
   at-home   e. travel writer
3. to **convene** for political reasons   a. agree   b. transgress
   c. assemble   d. disagree   e. part company
4. to **deviate** from habit   a. procrastinate   b. learn   c. hesitate
   d. stray   e. travel

Circle the letter of the best ANTONYM (the word or phrase most nearly opposite the word(s) in bold-faced type).

5. **impervious** to heat   a. sensitive   b. impenetrable   c. thankful
   d. unresponsive   e. translucent
6. a(n) **devious** plan   a. reliable   b. strange   c. straightforward
   d. ill-designed   e. rejected
7. to **intervene in** a quarrel   a. take part in   b. interfere in
   c. withdraw from   d. advise in   e. start
8. to **circumvent** the rules   a. avoid   b. ignore   c. relax   d. seek
   e. follow

EXERCISE 12B

Circle the letter of the sentence in which the word in bold-faced type is used incorrectly.

1. a. Pilots who **circumvent** airspace regulations fly at risk.
   b. **Circumventing** their supervisor, workers went straight to the
      company director with their complaint.
   c. To **circumvent** a quarrel we gave the twins identical presents.
   d. The children grew dizzy after **circumventing** on the merry-go-
      round.
2. a. Fearing foreign **intervention**, the Japanese closed their ports to
      Western trade until the mid-nineteenth century.
   b. Through the **intervention** of the goddess Athena, the travel-worn
      Odysseus returns to Ithaca.

    c. The gallery owner **intervened** photographs by Dorothea Lange between two by Ansel Adams.
    d. Parents must sometimes **intervene** when children quarrel.
3. a. **Telepathy** is a form of extrasensory perception.
    b. The first transatlantic cable was laid to assist intercontinental **telepathy**.
    c. Sometimes coincidence is mistaken for **telepathy**.
    d. In Madeline L'Engle's *A Ring of Endless Light* Vicky Austin has the **telepathic** power to communicate with dolphins.
4. a. She **deviated** from the modern language requirement by taking four years of Latin.
    b. Tired of freeways, the driver **deviated** the back roads.
    c. Normal children may **deviate** substantially from what are considered average growth patterns.
    d. Migrating birds rarely **deviate** from the flight path that they have followed in previous seasons.
5. a. The film *If It's Tuesday This Must Be Belgium* parodies a too rapid **itinerary** through too many countries.
    b. The Air and Space Museum in Washington, D.C., is an **itinerary** you should not miss.
    c. Aviator Amelia Earhart's planned **itinerary** around the globe in 1937 was interrupted when her plane disappeared over the Pacific Ocean.
    d. Mary Kingsley became famous as traveler and lecturer by describing the adventure and dangers of her West African **itinerary** in 1894 and 1895.

EXERCISE 12C   Fill in each blank with the most appropriate word from Lesson 12. Use a word or any of its forms only once.

1. The _____ of the space age has speeded up the gathering of information about our universe.
2. The airline pilot took a southerly route to _____ the electrical storm over Kansas.
3. Blizzards and dust storms often forced westbound pioneers to _____ from recommended routes.
4. To settle disputes between scientists and animal rights activists, the university _____d a bilateral meeting.
5. Alejandro Malaspina's _____ from Spain to the northwest coast of North America included stops in Chile and Peru.
6. This new carpet is _____ to stains.

REVIEW EXERCISES FOR LESSONS 11 AND 12

1 Fill in the blank or circle the letter of the best answer.

1. transient : itinerant ::
   a. ambience : atmosphere
   b. deviation : adventure
   c. telepathy : intervention
   d. deviousness : honesty
   e. itinerary : destination
2. *hodos* : *tele* ::
   a. aberration : suffering
   b. where : way
   c. way : journey
   d. journey : at a distance
   e. today : in the past
3. *ad*vent : to ::
   a. *de*viate : into
   b. *circum*vent : with
   c. *inter*vene : away from
   d. *ex*odus : around
   e. *trans*lucent : across
4. Which pair does not match the relationship of the first pair in root and its meaning?
   ab*erra*tion—wander
   a. ob*itu*ary—die
   b. circum*vent*ion—come
   c. epis*ode*—journey
   d. trans*gress*ion—step
   e. trans*it*ive—go
5. Which one of these pairs does not come from the same root?
   a. impervious—deviate
   b. aberration—erratic
   c. transitive—telepathy
   d. convene—advent
   e. ambience—transient

6. *Hodos* and *iter* both mean _____.

7. Many English words are derivatives from *venire*, meaning _____,

   and *ire*, meaning _____.

2 Writing or Discussion Activities

1. Imagine that on your way to school you have an experience
    suggested by each of the words listed below. Write a sentence or two
    describing each situation with such detail that you do not need to
    use the word in your description. Let the action explain the
    meaning.
    a. transgress
    b. intervene
    c. deviate
    d. convene
2. If you encountered books bearing these titles, how much could you
    tell about the contents of each one? Explain in a sentence or two
    what sort of information each would contain.
    a. *The Case of the Devious Itinerant* (mystery)
    b. *The Advent of Telepathy* (science fiction)
    c. *Our Erratic Exodus* (travel)
    d. *It's Only a Transitory Aberration* (advice)
3. If you were to write your autobiography it might include a
    description of a move you have made to another house, another
    school, or another place. Write a paragraph in which you use lots of
    details to describe the move you made, the reasons for it, and your
    feelings about it. If you have stayed in one place, choose a travel
    experience: being in a part of town or a place unfamiliar to you.
    Describe the situation, your reasons for being there, and your
    feelings about the episode. Use at least four words from Lessons 11
    and 12.
4. The motto *Vade mecum*, which begins this lesson, has been adopted
    into English, meaning "something used for reference that you carry
    with you" in a pocket, bookbag, or purse. A vade mecum may be a
    small book, such as a pocket dictionary, a calculator, a photograph,
    or other object. Write a sentence or two describing a vade mecum
    that you habitually carry with you.

Sports

LESSON 13

Tempus ludendi.
A time for playing.

Key Words

abject	conglomeration	interjection
accelerate	conjecture	precursor
celerity	discourse	succor
concur	incur	

Familiar Word
decelerate

Challenge Words
accelerando
accelerometer

CELER <L. "swift"

1. **accelerate**   (ĕk sĕl'ə rāt´)   [*ac* = *ad* <L. "to"]
   tr. and *intr. v.* To cause faster movement; to go faster.

   Heat caused the chemical reaction to **accelerate**.

   acceleration, *n.*

2. **celerity**   (sə lĕr´ə tē)
   n. Swiftness; quickness; speed.

   Atalanta, outrunning all but one who challenged her in a footrace, is a mythological example of **celerity**.

Familiar Words
corridor
course
current
cursive
cursor
excursion
occur
occurrence
recur
recurrence

Challenge Words
courier
cursory
hussar
recourse

CURRO, CURRERE, CUCURRI, CURSUM <L. "to run"
CURSOR, CURSORIS <L. "runner"

3. **concur** (kən kûr′) [*con = cum* <L. "with"]
   intr. v. 1. To agree; to cooperate.

   Conflicts arise when parents do not **concur** on methods of child-rearing.

   2. To coincide; to happen simultaneously.

   In Shakespeare's plays human violence often **concurs** with storms and earthquakes.

   concurrence, *n.*; **concurrent**, *adj.*; **concurrently**, *adv.*

4. **discourse** (dĭs′kôrs′, dĭs kōrs′) [*dis* <L. "apart," "in different directions"]
   n. 1. Conversation.

   Before the advent of movies and television, lively **discourse** was a popular amusement.

   2. A formal discussion of a subject in speech or writing.

   Published in 1543, Copernicus's **discourse** on the orbit of the sun provided the basis for modern astronomy.

   intr. v. To talk; to discuss formally in speech or writing.

   Sometimes considered the most learned American woman of the nineteenth century, Margaret Fuller could **discourse** with scholars on both sides of the Atlantic.

5. **incur** (ĭn kûr′) [*in* <L. "in"]
   tr. v. To meet with; to run into; to bring upon oneself.

   The Greek hero Odysseus **incurred** the anger of the giant Polyphemus by poking out his single eye with a burning stick.

   incursion, *n.*

6. **precursor** (prĭ kûr′sər, prē′kûr′ sər) [*pre* <L. "before"]
   n. Forerunner.

   The **precursor** of American baseball is the English game of rounders.

   precursory, *adj.*

7. **succor**   (sŭk′ər)   [*suc = sub* <L. "under"]
   n. Help in time of distress.

   The Red Cross, founded by Clara Barton in 1881, gives **succor** to victims of flood, fire, and famine.

   tr. v. To render help to.

   To **succor** her needy family, Jo March writes stories for magazines and even sells her hair in the novel *Little Women*.

GLOMUS <L. "ball"

8. **conglomeration**   (kən glŏm′ə rā′shən)   [*con = cum* <L. "with"]
   n. A collection of unrelated things.

   At the flea market we sifted through a **conglomeration** of tools, lamps, jewelry, and clothing.

   conglomerate, *n.* and *adj.*

JACIO, JACERE, JECI, JACTUM <L. "to throw"

Familiar Words
adjective
dejected
eject
inject
object
project (*n.* & *v.*)
subject (*n.* & *v.*)

9. **abject**   (ăb′jĕkt, ăb jĕkt′)   [*ab* <L. "away from"]
   adj. 1. Humiliating and miserable.

   Slaves on their way to the Americas endured **abject** conditions in crowded, disease-ridden ships.

   2. Contemptible.

   Those who kill baby seals to sell their skins are **abject** in the eyes of animal lovers.

   abjection, *n.*; **abjectly**, *adv.*

Challenge Words
adjacent
projectile
subjective
trajectory

10. **conjecture**   (kən jĕc′chər)   [*con = cum* <L. "with"]
    n. An opinion formed from inconclusive evidence; a guess.

    The number of galaxies in the universe is still a matter of **conjecture**.

    tr. and *intr. v.* To conclude from insufficient evidence.

    People have **conjectured** for centuries about the fate of the lost civilization of Atlantis.

11. **interjection**   (ĭn tĕr jĕk′shən)   [*inter* <L. "between"]
    n. A word or phrase sometimes inserted between other words,
    often expressing emotion; a word not linked grammatically to
    other words in a sentence.

    "Oh!" and "Ouch!" are **interjections**.

    interject, *v.*

EXERCISE 13A   Circle the letter of the best SYNONYM (the word or phrase most nearly
the same as the word in bold-faced type).

1. to **discourse** on many subjects   a. be informed   b. converse
   c. meditate   d. concur   e. grow long-winded
2. **abject** poverty   a. uplifting   b. wretched   c. endurable
   d. undeserved   e. severe
3. the **celerity** of their response   a. rudeness   b. emotion
   c. conditions   d. quickness   e. importance
4. a **conglomeration** of artifacts   a. creator   b. box   c. painter
   d. collector   e. collection

Circle the letter of the best ANTONYM (the word or phrase most nearly
opposite the word in bold-faced type).

5. **accelerated** the pace   a. rushed   b. slowed   c. ignored
   d. recorded   e. quickened
6. a famous **precursor**   a. forerunner   b. successor   c. champion
   d. writer   e. sprinter
7. an unwelcome **interjection**   a. explosion   b. grammar lesson
   c. sudden word   d. long discourse   e. interference

EXERCISE 13B   Circle the letter of the sentence in which the word in bold-faced type is used incorrectly.

   1. a. The one-time millionaire **incurred** financial ruin.
       b. After studying hard, teenagers like to **incur** their friends and relax.
       c. News reports told us about an **incursion** of Laotian troops into Cambodia.
       d. Snobbery in a new employee may **incur** resentment.
   2. a. Great literature offers **succor** to readers through interpretation of universal problems.
       b. In the Biblical story the Good Samaritan takes a risk when he gives **succor** to a stranger.
       c. A Scottish woman known in San Francisco's Chinatown as the White Devil **succored** girls by rescuing them from slavery.
       d. When the shark took a large bite from the surfboard, the surfer shouted, "**Succor!**"
   3. a. The people trapped at the top of the burning building **conjectured** themselves into the nets below.
       b. That the world's climate is changing because of the "greenhouse effect" is still only **conjecture**.
       c. Some scientists **conjecture** that a tenth planet may be orbiting the sun every 700 to 1,000 years.
       d. Can you **conjecture** what your life will be like in ten years?
   4. a. Although the frightening creatures in *Where the Wild Things Are* at first stirred controversy, readers of all ages now **concur** in the excellence of the book.
       b. After much bitter **concurring** the family finally agreed on an itinerary from Seattle to Denver.
       c. The **concurrence** in 1989 of movements in Europe toward democracy after decades of communist rule surprised political observers.
       d. The large theater provides **concurrent** showings of eight different films.
   5. a. When being introduced to royal personages one should be **abject** and either curtsy or bow.
       b. Millhands in nineteenth-century Britain worked in **abject** conditions with long hours and low pay.
       c. At the conclusion of World War I, Germany was **abject** in defeat.
       d. After the Armenian earthquake, victims suffered **abjectly** from their loss of food, shelter, and family.
   6. a. In desert regions a season's first heavy rainfall sharply **accelerates** the life of plants, sending them into a frenzy of growing.
       b. Invading Spain in 711, the Moors **accelerated** the development of literature, science, and the arts to heights never surpassed in recorded history.

c. **Accelerating** their voices, the cheerleaders could be heard throughout the stadium.

d. **Acceleration** of winds from the hurricane sent high tides crashing on lowland beaches.

EXERCISE 13C   Fill in each blank with the most appropriate word from Lesson 13. Use a word or any of its forms only once.

1. In antique shops you can find a(n) _____ of objects ranging from costly artifacts to useless junk.

2. Postal services promise _____ and care in mail delivery.

3. In the sentence, "Wow! What a victory," the word *wow* is a(n) _____.

4. The parents felt _____ despair when they discovered their child missing from the campground.

5. Racers in the Indianapolis 500 must _____ quickly and maintain high speed throughout the 500-mile course.

6. "Right and victory do not always _____."
    —John Selden

LESSON 14

Audaces fortuna juvat.
Fortune favors the bold.

Key Words		
assail	evolve	resilient
avail	exult	salient
convalesce	prevalent	valor
desultory		voluble

SALIO, SALIRE, SALUI, SALTUM <L. "to jump," "to leap"

1. **assail** (ə sāl′) [*as* = *ad* <L. "to"]
    tr. v. 1. To attack violently; to assault.

Familiar Words
insult
result
somersault

Challenge Words
salacious
sally
sauté

Mistaking distant windmills for unfriendly giants, the legendary Don Quixote **assails** one of them with his lance.

2. To attack with words; to ridicule or criticize harshly.

Movie reviewers may keep audiences away if they **assail** a film too harshly.

assailant, *n.*

2. **desultory**   (dĕs´əl tōr´ē, dĕs´əl tôr´ē)   [*de* <L. "down from"]
adj. 1. Jumping from one thing to another; rambling.

After hearing five **desultory** oral book reports, the class rejoiced when the bell rang.

2. Haphazard or random.

After a **desultory** search for the lost ball, the golfers gave up.

3. **exult**   (ĕg zŭlt´, ĭg zŭlt´)   [*e = ex* <L. "from," "out of"]
intr. v. To rejoice greatly; to be triumphant.

Althea Gibson **exulted** when she won the Wimbledon crown in 1957.

exultant, *adj.*; **exultantly**, *adv.*; **exultation**, *n.*

4. **resilient**   (rĭ zĭl´yənt, rĭ zĭl´ē ənt)   [*re* <L. "back"]
adj. 1. Capable of returning to the original shape after being bent or stretched.

Rubber is a **resilient** material.

2. Buoyant; recovering quickly from illness, change, or misfortune.

The **resilient** Lance Armstrong has won the Tour de France four times since surviving cancer in 1996.

resilience, *n.*

5. **salient**   (sā´lē ənt)
adj. 1. Conspicuous; striking.

The **salient** landmark in St. Louis is the Gateway Arch.

2. Projecting up or out.

The roofs of Chinese pagodas curve up, ending with **salient** figures such as dragons.

saliently, *adv.*

VALEO, VALERE, VALUI, VALITUM <L. "to be strong"

6. convalesce (kŏn´və lĕs´) [*con = cum* <L. "with"]
intr. v. To recover health after illness.

Until this century a tuberculosis patient would expect to **convalesce** slowly in a sanitarium for a year.

convalescence, *n.*

7. avail (ə vāl´) [*a* <Middle English intensifier]
tr. v. To use to one's own advantage (to *avail* oneself of).

The salient characteristic of the young heroes of Horatio Alger's stories is the ability to **avail** themselves of every chance to prosper.

NOTA BENE: As a noun, *avail* also means "benefit" or "advantage," usually in a phrase such as "to no *avail*."

8. prevalent (prĕv´ə lənt) [*pre* <L. "before," "forth"]
adj. Widely occurring or in general use.

Destruction of rain forests continues to be **prevalent**, causing harmful changes in weather around the globe.

prevail, *intr. v.*; **prevalence**, *n.*

9. valor (văl´ər)
n. Heroic courage; bravery.

A British nurse executed by firing squad during World War I, Edith Cavell proved her **valor** by protecting Allied soldiers from discovery.

valorous, *adj.*

VOLVO, VOLVERE, VOLVI, VOLUTUM <L. "to revolve"

10. evolve (ĭ vŏlv´) [*e = ex* <L. "from," "out of"]
intr. v. 1. To develop gradually.

The book as we know it **evolved** from handwriting on papyrus to printing with movable type, a process invented by Johann Gutenberg.

2. To change from a simpler to a more complex form of animal or plant life.

Challenge Words
circumvolve
convoluted
devolve
involution

Biologists propose that all living things have **evolved** to their present forms through successive generations.

evolution, *n.*; **evolutionary**, *adj.*

11. **voluble** (vŏl′yə bəl)
adj. Speaking in a steady, easy flow of words; talkative; glib.

Parents often become **voluble** when explaining how things were when they were young.

volubility, *n.*; **volubly**, *adv.*

EXERCISE 14A

Circle the letter of the best SYNONYM (the word or phrase most nearly the same as the word(s) in bold-faced type).

1. a show of **valor**   a. weakness   b. physical strength   c. celerity
   d. heroism   e. imagination
2. **exulted in** victory   a. worried about   b. grieved over
   c. participated in   d. rejoiced about   e. ignored
3. the **resilient** trampoline   a. springy   b. soft   c. inflexible
   d. slippery   e. salient

Circle the letter of the best ANTONYM (the word or phrase most nearly opposite the word in bold-faced type).

4. a **voluble** prizewinner   a. wordy   b. fidgety   c. chatty   d. brief
   e. tongue-tied
5. a long **convalescence**   a. deterioration of health   b. illness
   c. hospitalization   d. muscle-tightening   e. healing process
6. a(n) **prevalent** attitude   a. commonsense   b. backward-looking
   c. unhealthful   d. rare   e. usual

EXERCISE 14B

Circle the letter of the sentence in which the word in bold-faced type is used incorrectly.

1. a. At press conferences journalists **assail** the president with questions.
   b. In 1775 American forces **assailed** Fort Ticonderoga and defeated the British.
   c. The ships **assailed** through the Strait of Magellan, at the southern tip of South America.
   d. Jessica Mitford has **assailed** the funeral industry for taking monetary advantage of bereaved families.

2. a. Our process of thinking is usually **desultory** as we leap in an instant from one thought to another.
    b. The tornado moved **desultorily**, leaving a path of rubble.
    c. Be wise; don't be **desultory** in doing your homework.
    d. Angry words put one's friends into a **desultory** sulk.
3. a. Fashion sometimes dictates **salient** skirts.
    b. The **salient** hazard for ships in the North Atlantic is the iceberg, as the sinking of the *Titanic* illustrates.
    c. A **salient** wooden figurehead of a woman adorned the bow of the old sailing ship.
    d. The **salient** fact about Methuselah is that according to the Bible he lived for 969 years.
4. a. Supersonic planes have **evolved** from the Wright brothers' successful flying machine.
    b. Although reached independently, the **evolutionary** theories of Charles Darwin and Alfred Wallace concurred.
    c. Passengers on the famous train, the Orient Express, depart from Paris and **evolve** in Budapest.
    d. Albert Einstein's theory of relativity **evolved** from mathematical calculation and understanding of natural forces in the world.
5. a. Some experimenters known as alchemists labored in the Middle Ages to make gold from lesser metals, to no **avail**.
    b. Deprived of books in his youth, Richard Wright hungrily **availed** himself of library privileges by using a borrowed card.
    c. Early American pioneers **availed** themselves of free land by "squatting".
    d. Sandbaggers rushed to **avail** when the flood waters rose.

EXERCISE 14C

Fill in each blank with the most appropriate word from Lesson 14. Use a word or any of its forms only once.

1. Although my brother complained about the shortage of summer

    jobs, he had made only _____ attempts to find one.

2. The Spanish practice of branding cattle and horses was

    _____ in Mexico as early as the sixteenth century.

3. Despite the loss of her life's work in a fire, the artist remained

    _____ in spirit.

4. Pinocchio and Cyrano de Bergerac are two fictional characters who

    have in common one _____ feature: a very large nose.

5. The character of Fanny Flinching in *Little Dorrit* is so _____ that, according to her creator, her speech "has no commas in it."

REVIEW EXERCISES FOR LESSONS 13 AND 14

1 Circle the letter of the best answer to the following analogies and questions about roots and definitions.

1. guess : agree ::
   a. avail : prevail
   b. conjecture : concur
   c. incur : exult
   d. evolve : discourse
   e. convalesce : avail
2. precursor : forerunner ::
   a. abject : proud
   b. voluble : silent
   c. assailant : attacker
   d. available : unhandy
   e. resilience : celerity
3. concur : *currere* ::
   a. *glomus* : conglomeration
   b. prevalent : *volvere*
   c. succor : *celer*
   d. salient : *jacere*
   e. exult : *salire*
4. Which word is *not* derived from a Latin root meaning "jump" or "run"?
   a. incur
   b. salient
   c. resilient
   d. conjecture
   e. precursor
5. Which word does *not* have any meaning related to "speaking"?
   a. discourse
   b. convalescence
   c. conjecture
   d. voluble
   e. interjection

2   Writing or Discussion Activities

1. All of the words listed below come from *salire*, meaning "to jump."
    Choose one word and write a paragraph in which you guess at the
    connection between the English word and its Latin root.
    a. assail
    b. desultory
    c. exult
    d. resilient
    e. salient

2. Write a sentence in which you apply the word *celerity* to something
    that you do. In your sentence include the word and a specific
    situation.

3. On a camping trip, would you like to have along a person who can
    be described by the following words? Write a sentence for each
    word, explaining specifically why such a person would or would not
    be a good fellow-camper. Use the words in your sentences.
    a. resilient
    b. voluble
    c. desultory
    d. valorous

4. Write a sentence for each pair of words below. Create a specific
    situation from literature, history, your own experience, or your
    imagination.
    a. precursor—evolve
    b. discourse—interjection
    c. conglomeration—desultory

LESSONS 15 AND 16

Animals

LESSON 15

Ubi mel, ubi apes.
Where there is honey, there are bees.—PLUTUS

Key Words		
apiary	canine	capricious
aviary	caper	equestrian
bovine	caprice	equine
		equitation

APIS <L. "bee"

1. **apiary**   (ā′pē ĕr′ē)
   n. A place where hives or colonies of bees are kept for their honey.

   Since bees depend on sunlight to set their flight bearings, an **apiary** should be located with its entrance facing east.

   apiarist, *n.*

AVIS <L. "bird"

2. aviary   (ā'vē ĕr´ē)
n. A house, enclosure, or large cage for birds.

Vibrantly colored parrots strutted inside the **aviary**.

aviarist, *n.*

BOS, BOVIS <L. "cow," "ox"

3. bovine   (bō'vīn, bō'vēn)
adj. Having the quality of a cow or ox: sluggish, dull.

Despite the comedian's antics, the audience sat in **bovine** silence.

bovinity, *n.*

CANIS <L. "dog"

4. canine   (kā'nīn)
n. Member of the family of dogs.

Like dogs, wolves and foxes are **canines**.

adj. Pertaining to the family of dogs, and especially the qualities associated with them.

Two **canine** movie stars are the faithful Rin Tin Tin and Lassie.

NOTA BENE: *Canine* is also used to refer to the eyetooth, between the incisor and the bicuspid. The word is used as both noun and adjective. Example: The child wears braces to realign protruding *canines*, or to realign *canine* teeth.

caninity, *n.*

| **Familiar Word** |
| Capricorn |

CAPER (m.), CAPRA (f.) <L. "goat"

5. **caper** (kā′pər)
   n. 1. A playful hop, leap, or skip.

   The colorful streamers of the maypole and the agile **capers** of the dancers contributed to the festive ambience of an English May Day.

   2. A prank or wild escapade.

   Mr. Toad's motor-car-stealing **caper** begins with easy acceleration and ends with wheels churning up mud in a horsepond.

   intr. v. To leap, frolic, or frisk about.

   The children **capered** excitedly when their kites began to soar.

| **Challenge Words** |
| capriccio |
| capriole |

6. **caprice** (kə prēs′)
   n. A sudden impulse, whim, or unmotivated change of mind.

   Hating changes, cartoon character Charlie Brown dreads the **caprices** of his friend Lucy.

   NOTA BENE: In music, a *caprice* is a lively instrumental work with a free form.

7. **capricious** (kə prĭsh′əs)
   adj. Subject to whim; impulsive; unpredictable or fickle.

   Popularity is **capricious**: yesterday's "insiders" are often on the outside today.

   capriciously, *adv.*; **capriciousness**, *n.*

EQUUS <L. "horse"

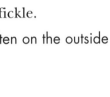

| **Challenge Word** |
| equerry |

8. **equine** (ē′kwīn)
   adj. Pertaining to a horse; belonging to the family of horses and zebras.

   Rosa Bonheur, nineteenth-century painter of animals, used **equine** subjects in her huge painting, "Horse Fair."

9. **equitation** (ĕk′wə tā′shən)
   n. The art of riding horses.

   In the Middle Ages a knight was expected to become a master of **equitation**.

10. **equestrian**   (ĭ kwĕs′trē ən)

adj. Pertaining to a rider of horses, or skill in riding.

An accomplished **equestrian** competitor, Robyn Smith was the first woman jockey to win a race involving major stakes.

n. One who rides or performs on horseback.

The Spaniards easily conquered the Americas not only because they were expert **equestrians**, but also because the native peoples had never before seen horses.

equestrianism, *n.*

EXERCISE 15A   Circle the letter of the best SYNONYM (the word or phrase most nearly the same as the word in bold-faced type).

1. a keeper of **apiaries**   a. monkey cages   b. honeycombs   c. worker bees   d. beehives   e. birds' nests
2. the **aviary** at the zoo   a. collection of beehives   b. large birdhouse   c. flying fish   d. exotic bird   e. butterfly specimens
3. to **caper** in the park   a. dance   b. sleep   c. leap   d. act on impulse   e. jog

Circle the letter of the best ANTONYM (the word or phrase most nearly opposite the word in bold-faced type).

4. a(n) **capricious** decision   a. whimsical   b. impulsive   c. emotional   d. clever   e. thoughtful
5. a **bovine** existence   a. peaceful   b. dull   c. lively   d. cheerful   e. rural

EXERCISE 15B   Circle the letter of the sentence in which the word in bold-faced type is used incorrectly.

1. a. Dressage[1] is a form of **equestrian** competition that requires subtle guidance of a horse through complex maneuvers.
   b. **Equestrian** troops are inefficient in modern warfare.
   c. A race horse can be trained to be an obedient **equestrian**.

---

[1]Usually pronounced drĕs ȧjh′.

d. In the Louvre in Paris you can see a ninth-century **equestrian** statue of the French Emperor Charlemagne as well as the portrait of Mona Lisa.

2. a. Spot could never be trained out of the **canine** drive to hunt rabbits.

b. Odysseus's aged dog Argos, who recognizes his master after an absence of twenty years, may be the most famous **canine** in ancient literature.

c. Barbara Woodhouse gained fame on television for her efficacious techniques in training the most ill-tempered **canines**.

d. The **canine** tricks of my canary entertain me constantly.

3. a. **Capricious** winds endangered the balloonists crossing the Atlantic Ocean.

b. I bought the house because of its **capricious** walk-in closets.

c. **Capricious** treatment from Scarlett O'Hara is all too familiar to Ashley Wilkes and Rhett Butler in *Gone with the Wind*; they tire of her fickle, undependable behavior.

d. Is your plan to study Chinese a serious intention or a **capricious** whim?

4. a. The crowd cheered the **bovine** leaps and catches of the trapeze artists.

b. The sunbathers lay in a state of **bovine** inertia.

c. Use of **bovine** growth hormones to increase milk production in dairy herds has been assailed by some consumers.

d. The mayoral candidate's **bovine** nature drove voters to write in the name of the more energetic deputy mayor.

EXERCISE 15C   Fill in each blank with the most appropriate word from Lesson 15. Use a word or any of its forms only once.

1. Modern sailors are still at the mercy of _____ weather.

2. Until the twentieth century, women _____s usually rode sidesaddle to accommodate their long skirts.

3. A beekeeper will plan ways to keep a(n) _____ safe from killer bees, which can dominate colonies of the milder honey bees.

4. Two books that pay tribute to _____ spirit and sensitivity are *Black Beauty* and *The Black Stallion*.

5. In the wild, _____s move in packs, following a strong lead dog; in civilization, the animal's owner replaces the leader of the pack.

6. Although annoyed, the houseguests had to tolerate the early

morning _____s of the children.

LESSON 16

In pacem leones, in proelio cervi.
Be lions in peace; be deer in battle.

Key Words		
feline	piscine	simian
leonine	porcine	ursine
lionize	serpentine	zoology

FELIS <L. "cat"

1. **feline**   (fē′lĭn)
   n. A member of the family of cats, lions, tigers, and jaguars.

   One of the most beautiful **felines** is the Siberian tiger.

   adj. Belonging to the cat family; having characteristics of a cat, such as gracefulness and independence.

   Characters in the Broadway musical *Cats* display a wide range of **feline** qualities.

   felinity, *n.*

Familiar Words
Leo
leopard
lion
lioness
lionhearted

LEO, LEONIS <L. "lion"
LEON <G. "lion"

2. **leonine**   (lē′ə nīn)
   adj. Pertaining to a lion; having characteristics of a lion, such as fierceness and majesty.

   The shaggy-haired speaker roared at the interruption with **leonine** ferocity.

3. **lionize**   (lī′ə nīz)
   tr. v. To regard or treat a person as a celebrity.

   Audiences **lionized** English author Anthony Trollope when he came to America to read from his novels.

   lionism, *n.*; **lionization**, *n.*; **lionship**, *n.*

Familiar Word
Pisces

Challenge Word
piscatorial

PISCIS <L. "fish"

4. piscine   (pī sēn′, pĭs′ īn)
adj. Typical of fish.

Piscine eyes look only to the sides, not straight ahead.

piscinity, *n.*

NOTA BENE: Of the twelve signs of the zodiac, seven are animals. Those not mentioned in these lessons are *Aries*, "ram"; *Scorpio*, "scorpion"; *Cancer*, "crab"; and *Taurus*, "bull." (*Capricorn* means "goat's horn.")

Familiar Words
porcupine
pork

Challenge Words
pork barrel
porker
porky

PORCUS <L. "swine," "pig," "hog"

5. porcine   (pôr′sīn)
adj. Pertaining to or resembling a pig.

Miss Piggy the Muppet is proud of her **porcine** features.

porcinity, *n.*

SERPENS, SERPENTIS <L. "serpent," "snake"

6. serpentine   (sûr′pən tēn′)
adj. 1. Resembling a serpent in form or movement: sinuous; winding.

The Colorado River takes a **serpentine** course from Colorado to Mexico.

2. Having qualities of a serpent: subtle, sly, sometimes even evil.

Convinced by the con artists' **serpentine** persuasion, the gullible couple signed over their life savings.

SIMIA <L. "monkey," "ape"

7. simian   (sĭm′ē ən)
adj. Pertaining to or resembling an ape or monkey.

Biologists have discovered that human beings possess **simian** social instincts such as sharing of food.

n. An ape or monkey.

The most teachable **simian**, a chimpanzee, can learn human sign language.

simianity, *n.*

URSA <L. "bear"

8. ursine (ûr′sīn)

adj. Pertaining to or characteristic of a bear.

The **ursine** habit of hibernation allows the animal to sleep throughout the winter in a cave or hollow log.

ursinity, *n.*

ZOION (plural ZOA) <G. "living being," "animal"

9. zoology (zō ŏl′ə jē)   [*logy* = *logos* <G. "word," "speech"]
n. The science dealing with animals. (Also used as an adjective.)

Students of **zoology** learn about animal groups and the varying structures of animal forms.

zoologic, *adj.*; **zoological**, *adj.*; **zoologically**, *adv.*; **zoologist**, *n.*

NOTA BENE: The equivalent Latin form for "living being," "animal" is *animal, animalis.*

EXERCISE 16A

Circle the letter of the best SYNONYM (the word or phrase most nearly the same as the word in bold-faced type).

1. **simian** features   a. ape-like   b. humane   c. amusing   d. familiar   e. wrinkled
2. **feline** leaps   a. awkward   b. slow   c. risky   d. graceful   e. capricious
3. a **zoologist**   a. veterinarian   b. person who studies animal life   c. caretaker of a zoo   d. person who evaluates zoos   e. person who collects animals
4. having a **leonine** manner   a. kittenish   b. gentle   c. clumsy   d. youthful   e. fierce

Circle the letter of the best ANTONYM (the word or phrase most nearly opposite the word in bold-faced type).

5. to **lionize** a famous actor   a. paw   b. annoy   c. idolize   d. despise   e. misunderstand
6. an unmistakably **ursine** pace   a. light-footed   b. bear-like   c. clumsy   d. slow   e. heavy
7. a(n) **serpentine** path   a. snake-infested   b. frightening   c. straight   d. winding   e. itinerant

EXERCISE 16B   Circle the letter of the sentence in which the word in bold-faced type is used incorrectly.

1.   a. The wild boar is a **porcine** cousin of the domestic pig.
     b. The chef's specialty is a **porcine** with an apple in its mouth.
     c. **Porcine** contours may result when appetites become too hearty.
     d. George Orwell's **porcine** characters in *Animal Farm* resent Farmer Jones's power but overthrow it with a corrupt power of their own.

2.   a. **Piscine** and *fishy* can rarely be used as synonyms because *fishy* has so many more variations of meaning, like "suspicious" and "devious."
     b. A **piscine** partnership exists between the yellow clownfish and the sea anemone, which grants immunity from its poisonous tentacles to few other fish.
     c. In 1926 Gertrude Ederle became the first woman to swim the English Channel, a notable **piscine** accomplishment.
     d. **Piscine** habits and habitats are subjects included in *The Compleat Angler* by Izaak Walton, a noted sixteenth-century fishing expert.

3.   a. The **serpentine** design on the chairback represented a Chinese dragon.
     b. Emily Dickinson describes a chilling **serpentine** encounter with "a narrow fellow in the grass."
     c. Drivers in the Alps need courage and good brakes to negotiate the frequent **serpentine** turns.
     d. The timid **serpentine** darted into his hole.

4.   a. The **ursine** seal resembles a bear in the color and shagginess of its fur.
     b. Winnie the Pooh shares with his wild **ursine** counterparts a love of honey.
     c. With an **ursine** waddle the opossum crossed the grass.
     d. The child had a dainty **ursine** appetite.

5.   a. Some Americans tend to **lionize** British royalty.
     b. Too rich a diet **lionized** our cat.
     c. Sixties' groups such as the Beatles and the Supremes were **lionized** wherever they performed.
     d. Authors may enjoy being **lionized** but will still complain about the interruption of their work.

6.   a. Both Jane Goodall and Dian Fossey have contributed to our understanding of **simian** behavior in their studies of chimpanzees and gorillas.
     b. **Simians** are like human beings in having an opposable thumb.
     c. The creature's head was hidden in its **simian** coils.
     d. Charles Darwin's theories showing human and **simian** similarities horrified many people in the nineteenth century because of conflict with religious beliefs.

EXERCISE 16C   Fill in each blank with the most appropriate word from Lesson 16. Use a word or any of its forms only once.

1. The dancer leaped with _____ coolness and grace.

2. _____ forms flickering in a coral reef thrill scuba divers.

3. In the study of _____ you will compare the structure and habits of birds, fish, and mammals.

REVIEW EXERCISES FOR LESSONS 15 AND 16

1 Matching: Apply what you have learned in these lessons about animals to the following new words, which appear in unabridged dictionaries. In the space at the left, write the letter of the phrase that defines the word in italics.

_____	**1.** *capric* acid	A. a beekeeper
_____	**2.** *piscivorous*	B. a place where serpents are kept
_____	**3.** *felicide*	C. fish-eating
_____	**4.** *apiarist*	D. the slaughter of birds
_____	**5.** *lionesque*	E. belonging to the family of oxen
_____	**6.** *serpentarium*	F. the constellation, Great Bear
_____	**7.** *bovoid*	G. smelling like a goat
_____	**8.** *canicular*	H. the act of killing a cat
_____	**9.** *Ursa Major*	I. like a lion
_____	**10.** *avicide*	J. referring to dog days (the period of hot weather in summer when the dog stars are visible in the night sky)

2 Writing or Discussion Activities

1. Write a sketch of a character from a book, movie, or TV show who possesses at least three of the following characteristics, usually uncomplimentary when applied to human beings. Use the words in your sentences, and show the specific ways in which the person is appropriately described: think of physical appearance, voice quality, movement, reactions, and habits.
   a. bovine
   b. capricious
   c. serpentine
   d. porcine

2. Write a character sketch using at least three of the words below, some of which will show favorable characteristics. Describe specific situations in which your invented character demonstrates qualities associated with the animals contained in the words. Use the words in your description.
   a. canine
   b. equine
   c. feline
   d. leonine
   e. piscine
   f. ursine

WORD LIST

(Numbers in parentheses refer to the lesson in which the word appears.)

aberration (11)
abject (13)
accelerate (13)
accrue (10)
advent (12)
ambience (11)
annihilate (4)
antebellum (7)
antecedent (7)
anterior (7)
aperture (4)
apiary (15)
artifact (9)
artifice (9)
artisan (9)
artless (9)
assail (14)
attenuate (5)
avail (14)
avant-garde (7)
aviary (15)

beneficence (10)
bicentennial (2)
bilateral (1)
bipartisan (1)
bisect (1)
bovine (15)

canine (15)
caper (15)
caprice (15)
capricious (15)
catholic (3)
celerity (13)
centenary (2)
centigrade (2)
circumvent (12)
cloister (3)
comply (5)
concur (13)
conglomeration (13)
conjecture (13)
context (10)
convalesce (14)
convene (12)
copious (6)
crescendo (10)

decathlon (2)
decimate (2)
depict (9)
desultory (14)
deviate (12)
devious (12)
discourse (13)
duplex (1)
duplicate (1)

efficacious (10)
episode (11)
equestrian (15)
equine (15)
equitation (15)
erratic (11)
evolve (14)
excrescence (10)
exodus (11)
expletive (5)
exult (14)

facile (10)
facsimile (10)
faction (10)
feline (16)

holocaust (3)

impervious (12)
implement (5)
incantation (9)
inception (4)
incipient (4)
incur (13)
interjection (13)
intervene (12)
itinerant (12)
itinerary (12)

leonine (16)
lionize (16)

macrocosm (6)
magnanimous (6)
magnate (6)
magnitude (6)
megalomania (6)
microbe (5)
microcosm (5)
minuscule (5)
minutia (5)
mollify (10)
monarch (1)
monogram (1)
monolith (1)
monologue (1)
monopoly (1)

negate (4)
nihilism (4)

obituary (11)
ode (9)
omnipotent (3)
omnipresent (3)
omnivorous (3)
overt (4)

panacea (3)

pandemonium (3)

parody (9)

pictograph (9)

piscine (16)

polygamy (6)

polygon (6)

porcine (16)

posterior (8)

posthumous (8)

precept (7)

preclude (3)

precursor (13)

predestination (7)

preempt (7)

premier (8)

premonition (7)

preposterous (7)

pretentious (7)

pretext (10)

prevalent (14)

primate (8)

prime (8)

primeval (8)

primordial (8)

quadrant (2)

quartet (2)

quatrain (2)

recant (9)

recluse (3)

renegade (4)

replete (5)

resilient (14)

rhapsody (9)

salient (14)

satiate (5)

serpentine (16)

simian (16)

succor (13)

telepathy (12)

tenuous (5)

totalitarian (3)

transgress (11)

transient (11)

transitive (11)

transitory (11)

translucent (11)

trilogy (2)

trisect (2)

triumvirate (2)

unanimous (1)

unilateral (1)

ursine (16)

vacuous (4)

valor (14)

vanguard (7)

vanity (4)

vaunt (4)

voluble (14)

zoology (16)